HAPPY *Thursday*

B. Renee Collins, Ph.D.

ISBN 978-1-64515-094-7 (paperback)
ISBN 978-1-64515-095-4 (digital)

Christian Faith Publishing, Inc.
832 Park Avenue
Meadville, PA 16335
www.christianfaithpublishing.com

Printed in the United States of America

A Martyr to Noise

Today, several things come to mind as I sit in my office grading my senior education majors' portfolios from summer I's Dream-Catchers summer camp experiences. I notice there is absolute silence in our office area as well as in the hallways in our building. This is a rare experience, one that doesn't happen often.

A few things from different time periods of my past, regarding the stillness or absence of movement or sounds, come to mind:

- When our oldest child was an infant, he suffered from chronic colic. Remember these were the days prior to all the over-the-counter remedies that parents have available now, like gripe water; etc. Bob and I took turns constantly moving Bobby in a stroller, a swing, or just walking around at night for him to sense movement and go to sleep. One night, Bob finally had Bobby asleep after numerous attempts, moving around the house, including using the dryer's sound and movement. As Bob quietly tiptoed to the nursery across the old wooden floor that creaked as you stepped, Bob accidentally came too close to the side of the door with Bobby's head (which that is another story in itself). Immediately, there was crying from both by Bobby and Bob from the incident.

- After we moved to Abilene, Bob's grandmother, who lived in the Shreveport, Los Angeles area, came to visit us for three months. She attended numerous sports, church, and civic events here in Abilene with our family. Whenever she returned home to LA, she asked me to listen. I made the comment, "I don't hear anything." She responded, "Exactly.

There is no wind here like there is in Abilene." She said, "I love the stillness here at home."

- Hangs. Through the years of babysitting, we have either a German grandmother clock or a genuine Bavarian black forest cuckoo clock that hangs in our living room. Through the years of babysitting the grandchildren as infants, there is never a more deafening sound like one of the clocks going off right when you get a baby to sleep. Or another time that is quite noticeable is prayer time during a church prayer time during a church service in our home on Wednesday nights. Turning the sound off is one of the things on our checklist to do prior to people arriving to worship weekly in our home.

What does the Bible say about stillness?

"The LORD is in his holy temple; let all the earth be silent before him" (Habakkuk 2:20).

"He got up, rebuked the wind and said to the waves, "Quiet! Be still!" Then the wind died down and it was completely calm" (Mark 4:39).

"He made the storm be still, and the waves of the sea were hushed" (Psalm 107:29).

"The Lord your God is in your midst, a mighty one who will save; He will rejoice over you with gladness; He will quiet you by his love; He will exult over you with loud singing" (Zephaniah 3:17).

"Be still before the Lord and wait patiently for him; fret not yourself over the one who prospers in his way, over the man who carries out evil devices!" (Psalm 37:37)

What are you fretting about today? What is the storm that is surrounding you? Lift your eyes to the source of stillness. It is not a foreign idea or an impossibility. We make decisions all of the time. We choose to do the things we want to do. Someone recently asked me, "Renee, who makes your schedule?" I responded, "I do." She then said, "You have the power to change your schedule." This same friend later sends me this quote from Ralph Waldo Emerson, which reads, "Finish each day and be done with it. You have done what you could. Some blunders and absurdities no doubt crept in; forget them as soon as you can. Tomorrow is a new day. You shall begin it serenely and with too high a spirit to be encumbered with your old nonsense."

I choose not to be a martyr to the storms of life or things that try to flood my mind even when I recline. I desire to submit everything unto the Lord. I desire to be still and know that He is God. I want to focus on His plan for me. I desire to move at His direction and not be swayed, distracted, or persuaded to do anything else. Be still.

And It Came to Pass

Here are a few of my favorite significant moments of the Bible:

- Then God said
- And it came to pass
- Such a time as this

There are significant moments in my life that I felt like the verse stated, "And it came to stay…" I sometimes cry out to the Lord to wake Him up and ask if He cares about all that is occurring in my life. I hesitate or become paralyzed with worry or fear of the unknown. I speak from my emotions rather than from His words.

An education major stopped by my office this week and shared how she is holding on to two verses about things in her life. The visit was a confirmation of what I was wanting to write about this week. I wanted to focus on how things come to pass (whenever we follow His guidance and not our own), for the times we are currently positioned in difficult situations. It boils down to knowing, understanding, and applying the truth from the Lord (sounds a bit like Bloom's taxonomy of thinking—the education majors/educators know what I am referring). It's all about living out our faith in Him.

> As he got into the boat, his disciples followed him. And a great storm developed on the sea so that the waves began to swamp the boat. But he was asleep. So they came and woke him up saying, "Lord, save us! We are about to die!" But he said to them, "Why are you cowardly, you people of little faith?" Then he got up and rebuked the

winds and the sea, and it was dead calm. And the men were amazed and said, "What sort of person is this? Even the winds and the sea obey him!" (Matthew 8:23–27)

"Who can say but that God has brought you into the palace for just such a time as this?" (Esther 4:14).

Then God said, and it came to pass—for such a time as this.

As I take inventory of my life, I am blessed with confidence in certain areas of my life, yet I recognize the areas that I panic or worry about how to complete. Just as Esther had the queen's position, her true identity as a Jew was hidden or masked until a moment in time. She didn't realize who she was until she was given a challenge. It wasn't until she began to listen to her cousin's warning that she realized that her position as queen could be the only voice to change history for a group of people, as well as herself. She was willing to have her husband, the king, wave the golden scepter over her for the verdict of life or death for even voicing her thoughts about the situation. She probably thought about the many reasons why she should not speak to her husband, but she decided to pray for wisdom about the timing and the words to say. She did not hesitate to execute the plan once it was given to her from on high. Her decision to speak to the king became a pivotal moment in her life, as well as for the future of her people. It was an overwhelming time of her life, but she followed through with the conversation. It came to pass.

I need to recognize those situations in my life – He is allowing me to be in situations to walk out my faith in Him as well as share His love and grace to bring others to freedom – *for such a time as this.*

Near the end of the Book of Esther, chapter 8, verse 8, you read the following: "Then seal the order with the king's signet ring, because no letter written in the king's name and sealed with his signet ring can be canceled."

Who is our king? His orders can only be canceled by our free will. What is it that you want to come to pass? What place is God using you for such a time as this? Focus on His words only, not your own understanding.

Then God said and it came to pass for such a time as this.

And the Winner Is...

Here lately there has been a great deal of laughter about special emcees announcing the wrong winners, like the Miss Universe Pageant first place winner and the Academy Awards Best Movie Award. I imagine how both winners feel within the five to ten seconds of the sudden announcement. Everyone looks around for the reaction of the sudden winner and the second place winner immediately vanishes from the center of the stage. Things change so quickly. Events like these cause people's lives to change suddenly. How many times have you advanced to first place or received a blessing from the Lord?

My word of encouragement this week is to know your identity in Christ! Things change in a matter of seconds. You receive a phone call from a friend who states, "I'm paying for your airfare to attend your high school reunion in three months. Get your bags packed. Don't say no." You had pretty much given up on attending the reunion due to the timing and the money. On the other hand, you receive a wedding card with money two years after you get married. The gift of money is the exact amount of a bill that is due within the week. Someone suddenly remembered to congratulate you and your husband about getting married. The final bill due for your eighth grade son's trip to Washington DC is due, and you are not sure how to make the payment. You check the mail before you drive to school. One of your small investments has made a sudden profit; you receive a check in the mail that clearly covers the final payment for your son's trip. Think about the timing of the US Postal Service; the provision is coming to you to change things to first place.

The Lord hears our heart, and He responds with His timing. The bit of time before I see it in the flesh is a time of trusting and believing. I now add to that bit of time the ingredient of praise or gratitude before I see it happen. I am learning more each day about the importance of thanking the Lord before I see things happen. According to *Online Dictionary*, faith means complete trust or confidence in someone or something. I know who I am in Him. I know my benefits or inheritance because of my birthright.

"Giving thanks always and for everything to God the Father in the name of our Lord Jesus Christ" (Ephesians 5:20).

"Do not be anxious about anything, but in everything by prayer and supplication with thanksgiving let your requests be made known to God" (Philippians 4:6).

"Let us come into his presence with thanksgiving; let us make a joyful noise to him with songs of praise!" (Psalm 95:2)

Earlier my faith level is smaller, and later, because of my self-image. I feel like the second place winner rather than the first place winner. Occasionally, I feel I do not deserve any roses or the trophy. I sometimes let the voices of so many others describe my destiny rather than read, understand, and declare what the Lord says to me. I am not any of the things spoken about me by relatives, teachers, so-called friends, and colleagues.

Here is what I declare:

- I am a child of God.
- I am a joint heir with Jesus.
- I have been accepted by Christ.
- I am a new creature in Christ.
- I am His beloved.
- I am forgiven and set free.
- I have been blessed with every spiritual blessing in the heavenly places.

- I am chosen, holy, and blameless before God.
- I am created in His image.
- I am God's workmanship, created to produce good works.
- I have boldness and confident access to God through faith in Christ.
- I have been made complete by Christ.
- I have been chosen by God, and I am holy and beloved.

"And the winner is" no mistake this time. Well done, my good and faithful servant. He is the author and the finisher of my faith. His word does not return void. He makes no mistakes.

Body Armor of Christ

Recently, I observed a short news clip about clothing that guarantees no wounds if you are shot. This new concealable, bulletproof shirt is now for the person's everyday fashion rather than only for high profile personalities, soldiers, or law enforcement agents. Would this be something to give someone special as a future Christmas gift? What has our world come to these days?

Right now, many people are hurting physically, mentally, emotionally, as well as spiritually. They desire to run to a strong tower and be vindicated by someone. Many people want to clear the past and move forward with a clean slate. Therefore, so many people are infatuated with superheroes or superheroines. They want someone to come along and make things less painful, less difficult, or less—— (whatever you want to complete the blank). They want to live in a bulletproof world with no hurts, worries, anxieties, or problems.

Read the entire chapter of Psalm 91 and highlight the words that matter to you right now. For me, a few of the words that I am holding tightly to include verses 10–11: "No evil will fall upon you, and no affliction will approach your tent, for he will command his angels to protect you in all your ways." Write these words down and meditate on truth rather than the lies of the enemy. Let the word of God become real in your heart and mind. Profess these words rather than words from other voices around you. You do not have to fear.

> The one who lives in the shelter of the Most High,
> who rests in the shadow of the Almighty,
> will say to the Lord,
> "You are my refuge, my fortress,
> and my God in whom I trust!"

He will surely deliver you from the hunter's snare
and from the destructive plague.
With his feathers he will cover you,
under his wings you will find safety.
His truth is your shield and armor.

You need not fear terror that stalks[b] in the night,
the arrow that flies in the day,
plague that strikes in the darkness,
or calamity that destroys at noon.
If a thousand fall at your side
or ten thousand at your right hand,
it will not overcome you.
Only observe[c] it with your eyes,
and you will see how the wicked are paid back.

"Lord, you are my refuge!"

Because you chose the Most High as your dwell-
    ing place,
no evil will fall upon you,
and no affliction will approach your tent,
for he will command his angels
to protect you in all your ways.
With their hands they will lift you up
so you will not trip over a stone.
You will stomp on lions and snakes;
you will trample young lions and serpents.

The Lord Speaks
Because he has focused his love on me,
I will deliver him.
I will protect him[d]
because he knows my name.
When he calls out to me,
I will answer him.

I will be with him in his[e] distress.
I will deliver him,
and I will honor him.
I will satisfy him with long life;
I will show him my deliverance. (Psalm 91)

This new bulletproof body armor is basically found in Ephesians 6:10–18:

> Finally, be strong in the Lord, relying on his mighty strength. Put on the whole armor of God so that you may be able to stand firm against the Devil's strategies. For our struggle is not against human opponents, but against rulers, authorities, cosmic powers in the darkness around us, and evil spiritual forces in the heavenly realm. For this reason, take up the whole armor of God so that you may be able to take a stand whenever evil comes. And when you have done everything you could, you will be able to stand firm.
>
> Stand firm, therefore, having fastened the belt of truth around your waist, and having put on the breastplate of righteousness, and being firm-footed in the gospel of peace. In addition to having clothed yourselves with these things, having taken up the shield of faith, with which you will be able to put out all the flaming arrows of the evil one, also take the helmet of salvation and the sword of the Spirit, which is the word of God. Pray in the Spirit at all times with every kind of prayer and request. Likewise, be alert with your most diligent efforts and pray for all the saints.

Candlelight

You know we live in a world of standardized tests when a young child picks up a piece of trash in the classroom and asks the teacher "What do I do with this?" The teacher thinks about giving the child four options similar to a multiple-choice test. Option A: Throw on the ground. Option B: Hold until we go outside for recess. Option C: Throw in a circular container near the door. Option D: Place in your backpack.

Fortunately for me, life is not in a standardized test format. Although, occasionally, I prefer to have a set of choices to make a decision. I know that in my lifetime I even glanced in the sky for a rainbow to ensure that I had made a wise choice. Lately, a few people have asked for prayer about making the best choices in jobs, mates, and financial decisions. I shared with some of them about how my husband, Bob, and I use a mentality of praying and asking the Lord for a green or red light before pursuing things.

"But the wisdom that comes from heaven is first of all pure; then peace-loving, considerate, submissive, full of mercy and good fruit, impartial and sincere" (James 3:17).

"All this also comes from the Lord Almighty, whose plan is wonderful, whose wisdom is magnificent" (Isaiah 28:29).

If things are peaceable and fall into place without any of our orchestration after prayer, we believe the choice was the best for us at the time. If things are complicated and forced, then we decide to hold off or not do something. The Lord has always been faithful to lead if we follow through with seeking Him first. The "if-then" mind-set has been a key to unlock some major decisions in our lives and marriage.

One example involved me making a decision to strike with all of the public school teachers in south Mississippi in my earlier years of teaching. I disliked the current teacher pay, which was lower than the salaries in Puerto Rico, but I also felt that I signed a contract, agreeing to my salary. Who suffered through the five-day strike? The kids. As it turned out, after lots of prayer, I decided to drive through the picket line (no, I did not hit anyone!). As I crossed the line, I knew I felt peace with my decision. Later, I counted the cost, not in pay, but with friends, a few of those so-called teacher friends disappeared; and the true friends, who still stay in contact with me today, emerged with unconditional love. As an adult, I felt the repercussions of peer pressure. However, I knew that I had made the best decision for myself.

Here are a few more verses about seeking His ways and not our own:

"An intelligent heart acquires knowledge, and the ear of the wise seeks knowledge" (Proverbs 18:15).

"'For I know the plans I have for you,' declares the LORD, 'plans to prosper you and not to harm you, plans to give you hope and a future'" (Jeremiah 29:11).

"Your word is a lamp for my feet, a light on my path." (Psalm 119:105)

His word prevented me from stumbling numerous times or veering off the road He had designed for me. Sometimes I felt the lamp was more of a candle. Either way, His word illumined the obstacles and pitfalls along the way.

"My son, attend to my wisdom, and bow your ear to my understanding" (Proverbs 5:1).

In the beginning was the word and the word was God. I am in Him, and He is in me. Whenever I wake up, I renew my mind with His thoughts. I bow my ear to His understanding. The multiple-choice test format fades away. I walk carefully and peacefully in the candlelight.

Climate Change (a.k.a. Thy Kingdom Come)

Picture this: seventh grade math class; all desks in the classroom were pushed together in the center of the room; oh yes, the year is 1969 (yes, in the late sixties we sat in the old vintage school desks). Each school day, my friends and I raced to math class, not because of a great anticipation for learning but because we wanted to sit in the dead center of the class. She used a long stick, like a pool table stick, to jab anyone in the ribs if he/she did not know answers or answered incorrectly. Motivation to arrive early equals fear of receiving jabs in the ribs.

Another memory: undergraduate biology class, 1975, long rows of desks, podium in the center front, charts on the classroom walls, and the shiny tiled floor. The professor marched into the room, slammed a folder of notes on the podium along with her wristwatch, and proceeded to lecture without taking a breath. No one asked questions; you only wrote everything she said. There were no over-heads, no Promethean boards, no *TED Talks*, etc. There was only a transmission of information to all of us for a test. Motivation to excel equals fear of repeating the class.

Final memory: sixty years old, Abilene, Texas, loving husband, three amazing children and families, thirty-seven-year teaching career, many friends who have intersected my life through the military, the community, the schools, the university, and the church. My daily life involved a realization of hope, love, mercy, and grace through the power of Jesus Christ. I praised, meditated, and listened to the Greatest Teacher. Motivation to love equals His unconditional love for me.

Who set the atmosphere or climate in all three memories? Three teachers, two negative and one positive that is full of grace and truth.

Atmosphere is defined by the *Online Dictionary* as "the pervading tone or mood of a place."

Climate is defined by the *Online Dictionary* as "the prevailing attitudes, standards, or environmental conditions of a group, period, or place."

Recently, I heard an online message by Mark Batterson about the following idea: when many people suffer a *setback*, they tend to *step back* rather than realize that with God there is a way to *comeback*. I liked the way a few of my friends describe how that, with God, there is a shift in the atmosphere or climate around us, a hope, the confident expectation of good. Does hope prevail over hopelessness? Does victory prevail over feeling like a victim? Does worthiness prevail over feeling unworthy? What is the climate like in your mind and heart? Remember to daily renew your mind. With God there is always a comeback. He is about solutions, unity, forgiveness, acceptance, and love. It is not about us; it is always about Him. When we rehearse the goodness of God, the climate changes. Let us continue to pray "thy kingdom come, thy will be done on earth as it is in heaven." It cannot get any better than as it is in heaven.

"Watch over your heart with all diligence, for from it flow the springs of life" (Proverbs 4:23).

"Who has ascended into heaven and descended? Who has gathered the wind in His fists? Who has wrapped the waters in His garment? Who has established all the ends of the earth? What is His name or His son's name? Surely, you know!" (Proverbs 30:4)

Divine Labor

Currently, numerous people feel overwhelmed with deadlines, tests, projects, reports, and meetings. I hear brief and extended reasons for praying for the weekend, the Easter break, any possible snow days, or other types of cancellations. It is amazing how quickly the spring is racing by. We all know exactly how many weeks are remaining in the university semester or the academic year. We desire the summer and all that it involves.

Two words come to mind:

1. Work—activity involving mental or physical effort done in order to achieve a purpose or result (*English Oxford Online Dictionary*).
2. Rest—cease work or movement in order to relax, refresh oneself, or recover strength (*English Oxford Online Dictionary*).

Picture this: God praying for the seventh day after the first six days of creation. Here He is with the following job description:

1. Created day (light) and night (darkness)—heavens beyond the earth (Genesis 1:1–5)
2. Created the sky (atmosphere) and waters—(Genesis 1:6–8)
3. Created continents and islands (plant life)—(Gen. 1:9–13)
4. Created all stars and heavenly bodies–(Genesis 1:14–19)
5. Created all water life and life in air—(Gen. 1:20–23)
6. Created all dry land creatures and man/woman—(Gen. 1:24–31)

What did He do on the seventh day? *Rested*.

You need to consider the work of your hands. Is it pleasing? It is not wrong to feel good about your achievements. He knows we need time of refreshment. He desires for us to enjoy His creation. Have you thought about why we like to have plants or trees as part of our landscaping in our yards, or why we like to have plants or flowers in our apartment, house, offices, or residence halls? Why do we have a desire to have pets—a beta fish, a cat, a dog, a pony, or maybe a gecko? We all like to return to our roots of the Garden of Eden. These are the components of God's job description.

Why did He need rest? Some people believe He wanted to set an example of what we need to do. It is a time to connect with the Creator. No matter the reason, He set aside time to cease in the creation process. We need to set aside time to recreate (reminds us of recreation). Take care of yourself. Dedicate time to cease work, to recover strength. Look at your calendar. Find the intentional minutes, hours, or a day of rest. If it is good enough for the Creator, it is good enough for the creation, you.

Let go of stress. Find solutions rather than focus on problems. Prioritize important things versus urgent things. Review your personal mission statement, if you have one, such as why are you doing the things you are doing. Review the list of the six days of creation; He created everything in a specific sequence of importance. Everything is evolving; each creation needs the previous creation. Be wise in your decisions of your days and nights. Organize the events according to importance. Finally review everything. If it is good, rest.

Eat My Dust: Standing Tall

One of the most intriguing times for me in my twenty years of teaching was the first year that I taught a young fifth grade girl who was visually impaired. She had no eyesight at all. It was the first year ever that I gave a touch tour of my classroom. I had never thought about how precise my classroom arrangements were until I received the class list with her name and information. I knew that my aisles needed to be cord free, with no sharp objects on edges of counters or desks, and to make use of Braille labels, etc. I actually sat in various places of my classroom to see things from a new perspective, of one with no vision. Just to think in terms of what a dark world must be like and to rely on smells, touch, and sound affected me greatly. I also began to think about my typical language while teaching, no harm intended, but how much I referred to things related to vision, like "All eyes up front," "Good to see you," "I will see you tomorrow," "Look this way, please." Wow! What a highlighted season of time. Fortunately, we had no incidents that year when Heather's artificial eyeball fell out of its socket. I prayed consistently that year for safety, peace, and no fear.

New perspectives. It reminded me of a story in the Bible about a woman's perspective of constantly looking downward because she was bent over for eighteen years. Imagine the different incidents she faced, or should I say incidents that she strained to face. I am sure that constantly looking toward the ground provided her a continuous view of feet, clear or blocked paths, rodents scurrying by, trash, animal feces, and just pure plain dust everywhere. Everything in her life was difficult to do: eating, walking, sitting, resting, carrying things, or sleeping. There was no Extra Strength Tylenol or Bayer Arthritic Aspirin. She endured the pain and discomfort; however, she believed in this man who was going about doing good and healing people (Acts 10:38). She had heard the stories of this man who did not throw stones at people who had made mistakes but listened and loved people by sending them out to sin no more.

If you read the story about this unique woman in Luke chapter 13, you find out that she attended a synagogue one Sabbath day. Since she was bent over, it was probably easy to overlook her with everyone else standing or moving about with heads held high. She focused on the floor of the synagogue but listened intently to Jesus. The interesting description of the reason of her physical condition is in verse 11: "And a woman was there who had been crippled by a spirit for eighteen years. She was bent over and could not straighten up at all."

Interesting how Satan was cursed in the Garden of Eden in Genesis 3:14: "So the LORD God said to the serpent, 'Because you have done this, Cursed are you above all livestock and all wild animals! You will crawl on your belly and you will eat dust all the days of your life.'"

According to the *Merriam-Webster* online dictionary, dust means fine particles of matter (as of earth), particles that disintegrates into something, something worthless like a state of humiliation. The online *Bible Meanings* shares that the meaning of dust signifies that which is damned or the grave. This connects to various biblical references regarding dust:

- When Satan was condemned (Genesis 3:14)
- Dust to dust (Ecclesiastes 3:20)
- Placing dust on your head to represent grief and suffering (Lamentations 2:10)
- After destroying the golden calf, it became as dust (Deuteronomy 9:21)
- Shake the dust off of your feet if you are unwelcomed (Matthew 10:14)

This woman's view of the world was the same as Satan's—dust, or damnation. However, within her heart, her view of the world was of beauty for ashes, joy for mourning, peace for stress, energy for fatigue, standing tall for bending over because she had faith and knew about the redeemer. The demonic spirit could not stay within her when Jesus noticed her. Luke 13:12: "When Jesus saw her, he called her forward and said to her, 'Woman, you are set free from your infirmity.'"

Freedom indeed! Standing tall after eighteen long years just because He spoke the words to her. She had not performed anything to get healed. She had faith and believed. What do you believe today? What is your view of your world, defeat or victory? Do not waste any more time viewing your world from the ground. Look up and see where your help comes from. Stand tall. Tell Satan to eat your dust.

Essential Oil of God

Think back to some of your funniest memories with family or friends. I reflect on different time periods of my life, and I still laugh about certain things that happened as a child, teenager, young adult, wife, mom, teacher, and the "Nay Nay" phase (grandmother). Do not worry, I won't bore you with all of the stories. Just one.

Our family lived in a tall three-story apartment complex in Wiesbaden, Germany. The stairwells were lined with clean waxed terrazzo flooring. It was a common sound to hear someone falling down the stairs while taking groceries to an apartment, carrying laundry baskets to the basement, or maybe holding a small sleeping toddler to one of the six dwellings. I cannot recall the total times that someone in our family "bit the dust" or "crashed and burned" to the bottom landing near the exit of the building. This background knowledge is important for my story. One Sunday evening, Bobby, who was five years old, developed an extremely high fever and was not responding to any of the home treatments. I decided to take him to the USAF hospital ER. We sat in the waiting room for about an hour or so while different people entered the ER with various serious issues. One woman slowly limped in, holding her head. After she completed the paperwork with the nurse at the front desk, the injured woman plopped down in the seat next to me. As I was patting my son's back, reassuring him that he would soon see the doctor, I turned to the lady and noticed a huge knot on her forehead between her eyebrows. I thought she had fallen down her stairwell and injured herself. I sympathetically said, "My, you have a terrible knot on your forehead. I am sorry you fell." She quickly replied, "I am not here for that." Oh my! Thankfully, my son and I were called to see the doctor. You would not believe how many times I ran into that woman while grocery shopping or going through other military places until we transferred to Texas.

"Always laugh when you can. It is cheap medicine" (Lord Byron).

I needed to write about something light and humorous this week. I wanted to focus on joy, joyful things, being joyous, rejoicing, etc. Nehemiah 8:10 says that the joy of the Lord is our strength. It requires great strength to be joyful in times of stress, pain, loss, and fear.

> The Spirit of the Lord GOD is upon me, Because the LORD has anointed me To bring good news to the afflicted; He has sent me to bind up the brokenhearted, To proclaim liberty to captives And freedom to prisoners; To proclaim the favorable year of the LORD And the day of vengeance of our God; To comfort all who mourn, To grant those who mourn in Zion, Giving them a garland instead of ashes, The oil of gladness instead of mourning, The mantle of praise instead of a spirit of fainting So they will be called oaks of righteousness, The planting of the LORD, that He may be glorified. (Isaiah 61:1–3)

It is a choice, joy versus whatever (stress, fear, worry, or mourning). Think about Jesus, His entire life was a road map of joy that was set before Him. He counted it joy to suffer and endure the pain of the cross for everyone. We are even instructed to count it all joy to endure the various trials we face.

What causes the joy? Simply stated, gratitude. The sense of recognizing that all things are a result of grace, unmerited favor from God. When you think of the great exchange at the cross, joy overtakes any inward attention to problems, fears, lack, guilt, etc. Be grateful each day for what He did and is doing through you. Allow the oil of gladness to saturate your heart and the words to flow out of your mouth.

Feast or Famine: Word Up!

For some people life has become much easier with the many apps on the cell phone. The categories of life direct the consumer's choices. Here are a few of my favorite Pinterest boards: education, food and drink, DIY crafts, holiday and events, and home décor. A few other apps besides Pinterest that I have on my phone include the calendar, text, phone, Google, the Weather Channel, ESPN, YouTube, TV Guide, Facebook, and the Bible. Everything is at my fingertips as long as the phone is charged. It feels very freeing if I go somewhere without my phone or if my phone is not charged. I possess in the rectangular Android a feast of information; all I need to know is how to access the appropriate links or files for the situation at hand. I move from moments of famine or feast depending on the signal bars on the phone.

In the Old Testament, there were major and minor prophets that relayed messages from the Lord. During a particular time, a prophet named Amos spoke to the people about things that would happen in the future that is related to God's judgment. Amos, which means burden bearer, was a shepherd in the land of Tekoa near Jerusalem. He was not received by the religious people of the day because he was lacking the formal education of the time. His word consisted of judgment during a flourishing time of prosperity and immoral behavior. The people did not want to receive the warnings from Amos. The Lord was tired of lip service with no evidence of righteousness and justice from the hearts of the people. I wonder how many people would like to hear the following statement:

> "The days are coming," declares the Sovereign
> LORD, "when I will send a famine through the

land— not a famine of food or a thirst for water,
but a famine of hearing the words of the LORD.
(Amos 8:11)

How can you become more like Christ without feeding on
the word of God? In Matthew 4:4, we read, "Jesus answered, 'It is
written: "Man shall not live on bread alone, but on every word that
comes from the mouth of God.'"

Don't forget Hebrews 4:12: "For the word of God is alive and
active. Sharper than any double-edged sword, it penetrates even to
dividing soul and spirit, joints and marrow; it judges the thoughts
and attitudes of the heart."

If you desire to be more like Jesus, you need to feast on the
word, especially in the United States where the average American
possesses four Bibles per household. You have access to the word;
you do not require a priest or prophet to tell you what the Word
says.

"In the beginning was the Word, and the Word was with God, and
the Word was God" (John 1:1).

He is the author and finisher of your faith. His words direct
your path if you listen to His voice only. Do not allow the enemy to
hack into your heart and plant seeds of doubt, fear, confusion, or lies.
Feast on the Word and find out exactly who you are, what plans the
Lord has for you, and His nickname for you. He loves you.

Finish Line: Running versus Sprinting

This is the last week of class for students enrolled in the spring semester at Hardin-Simmons University. Next week involves final exams followed by the commencement. The prayer requests have increased, the caffeine intake has doubled for many, and the late hours have increased in the Richardson Library. I have talked to many students, faculty, and staff the past two weeks about how they are doing. The responses include descriptors like stress, anxiety, and fatigue. Everyone is ready for the finish line.

Picture a modern-day outdoor track with eight lanes. The eighth lane has about fifty additional meters. The inside lane covers four hundred meters. Therefore, to ensure fairness the runners, the starting time is staggered if the requirement is making a full loop of the track. I know two students in my classes this semester could explain more in depth about the process of running races. One of the students shared today about the amount of preparation to running a race.

I thought about the preparation and the actual race. I later learned that running is the art of pacing. I know that in teaching pacing is a major factor in the learning process—go too quickly, you lose your students; go too slowly, you lose your students. Like running, teaching requires the wisdom to know about how to sustain oneself and make adjustments as needed. Sometimes we sprint the shorter distances and lose energy. We become quite tired, frustrated, and disappointed. Guilt and condemnation fill our thoughts. As Christians, we are runners, people who go the long distances and pace ourselves in a way to finish the race.

How do we sustain ourselves and make the necessary adjustments in our walk with the Lord to finish the race He has before us?

"Therefore, since we are surrounded by such a great cloud of witnesses, let us throw off everything that hinders and the sin that so easily entangles. And let us run with perseverance the race marked out for us, fixing our eyes on Jesus, the pioneer and perfecter of faith. For the joy set before him he endured the cross, scorning its shame, and sat down at the right hand of the throne of God." (Hebrews 12:1–2)

Great cloud of witnesses: Who are those cheerleaders in your life? In my life, there are numerous people who celebrate with me, who push me in a positive manner, who listen to me dream, and who cry with me when I cry. These people are located in the stadium of the race, cheering me on to finish one more lap and to continue to the next goal. Surround yourself with positive people who share your dreams and goals. Shake the dust off those people who sabotage you and scheme to extinguish your dreams.

Throw off everything that hinders and easily entangles you: Make decisions that involve running the race the Lord has set before you and no one else. He does not promise a race without hurdles, but He does promise to give grace in order to clear the hurdles. He wants you to stay in your lane during the race. Renew your mind daily; focus on Him; and think about things that are pure, lovely, and just. Put on the whole armor of God; these are your racing clothes. Let His measurement of success guide you. Throw off the old and focus on the new creation that you are. Old things are passed on; behold all is new. The Lord has given you so much; the great exchange at the cross and the empty tomb seals the deal. Speak words of life, not death.

Fixing our eyes on Jesus: This is a simple yet powerful statement. Do we spend more time viewing ourselves during the race or on Jesus, the author and finisher of our faith? Isn't it interesting the word *author* in the Greek means captain, chief leader, or prince?

Read Acts 3:15: "You killed the author of life, but God raised him from the dead. We are witnesses of this."

When we look to Jesus, we forget our past and look toward the future, the goal. It is crucial to know *why* the Lord knitted you in your mother's womb. What is your purpose in this race? Fix your eyes on your author and finisher.

"No, dear brothers and sisters, I have not achieved it, but I focus on this one thing: Forgetting the past and looking forward to what lies ahead, I press on to reach the end of the race and receive the heavenly prize for which God, through Christ Jesus, is calling us" (Ephesians 3:13–14).

This race is almost finished. What is next?

Fixed Identity

One of the meanings of the word *planted*, according to the Online Dictionary is to place or fix in a certain position. One other interesting definition includes to station (a person) for the purpose of functioning in secret, as by observing, spying, or influencing behavior. In Bob's previous career as a federal agent with the US Air Force, he planted numerous people in positions as either a member in active duty or as a civilian in various settings in order to achieve the goal of infiltrating a massive operation. For some time, the plants needed a plausible background in case anyone attempted to check their identities. All parties involved in the planting of the fictitious person needed to go back through a fake biography as thorough as possible to ensure there were no gaps in the story. In this type of situation, the people who are committing a crime tend to be thorough researchers before accepting a new member into the group. The plants continued in that fake life for how much time that it required to bring down the group, or at least the major players in the group. No one was allowed to go off script until things were totally finished. The length of the undercover work for the person depended on the type of case Bob was assigned. Most of the time, the cases were successfully completed and taken to the appropriate courts in a rather short amount of time. However, there were several cases that required a great length of time, an endless amount of energy, and government funds to support everyone involved in protecting, monitoring, and supporting the plant.

"Blessed is the man who walks not in the counsel of the ungodly, nor stands in the path of sinners, nor sits in the seat of the scornful; but his delight is the law of the Lord, and in His law he meditates day and night. He shall be like a tree, planted by the rivers of water, that brings forth its fruit in its season, whose leaf also shall not wither; and whatever he does shall prosper" (Psalm 1:1–3).

Unlike the planted undercover person, someone who has made a decision to be fixed in Christ possesses a brand-new identity, one that is sealed. The new man is like a tree planted by the by the river. The river flows with unconditional love, grace, healing, forgiveness, righteousness, and peace from above. In Psalm 1:3, bringing forth fruit in its season reflects the perfect timing of the Lord. You cannot rush the growing of a fruit. Be patient and know the Lord is protecting, monitoring, and supporting you because you are fixed in Him. The last part of the verse shows how your constant meditation and delight in the law of the Lord produces prosperity. This means that you need to align your focus (mind-set) to things of the Lord, not your friends or your family.

The Lord's law given before the His crucifixion is different from the law given to Moses by God on Mount Sinai. Remember how the Lord says that His yoke is easy. Well, His yoke, or belief, is very different from memorizing a collection of "thou shalt nots." Matthew 22:37–39: "'You must love the Lord your God with all your heart, with all your soul, and with all your mind.' This is the greatest and most important[d] commandment. The second is exactly like it: 'You must love your neighbor as yourself.'"

How fixed are you near the river, by the river, away from the river, or in a desert with no river in sight? Time to trace your roots.

Forever Young

This week, I observed a couple of creative student teachers teaching history lessons in two different high school settings. As I was writing all of the wonderful things these two Hardin-Simmons University education majors were teaching, it hit me the time periods of history the HSU students were explaining to these sophomores and juniors in high school happened during my teen-aged years. I began to feel very old as the high school students made comments about the Vietnam War, the civil rights movement, things like the counter-culture music (e.g., Bob Dylan, Pink Floyd, Janis Joplin, etc.), mentioning flower power, and the idea of hippies, etc. One class of high school students shared how they had never heard of James Brown, the godfather of soul. For some of you reading this weekly encouraging note, you understood the shock I felt at this point.

Counterculture means the culture and lifestyle of those people, especially among the young, who reject or oppose the dominant values and behavior of society (*Merriam Online Dictionary*).

Now, I am proud to say that I am a member of the counterculture of our society in many areas, I am a believer in the culture of the Great I am—the deliverer, the redeemer, the advocate, the Prince of Peace—Jesus.

"Do not conform to the pattern of this world but be transformed by the renewing of your mind. Then you will be able to test and approve what God's will is--his good, pleasing and perfect will" (Romans 12:2).

"And to put on the new self, created to be like God in true righteousness and holiness" (Ephesians 4:24).

"But now, having died to what bound us, we have been released from the Law, so that we serve in the new way of the Spirit, and not in the old way of the written code" (Romans 7:6).

I remember a poster I had in my classroom for many years, "What is right is not always popular and what is popular is not always right" (Albert Einstein). Standing up for the truth is not easy whenever it is not popular. John 15:19: "If ye were of the world, the world would love his own: but because ye are not of the world, but I have chosen you out of the world, therefore the world hateth you."

Use the standard of the word of God, not man's opinions, to determine what you do, say, or believe. He is our rock, our fortress, a help in time of trouble. He is the same yesterday, today, and tomorrow. He is not the counterfeit.

"There is no one holy like the LORD, Indeed, there is no one besides You, Nor is there any rock like our God" (1 Samuel 2:2).

Gold, Silver, or Bronze?

Success is not final; failure is not fatal: It is
the courage to continue that counts.
—Winston S. Churchill

Here are a few clues about three people:

- One of twenty-one children, born prematurely, overcame polio by the age of twelve, won three gold medals in the Summer 1960 Olympics held in Rome, and coached underprivileged children after her retirement.
- One of twelve children, sold into slavery by family members, accused of sexual harassment, imprisoned, later given authority of agricultural decisions, stayed true in his faith, blessed in a position of influence, and later reunited with family.
- One of twelve children born in slavery, his mother died when he was six weeks old, he was a nameless orphan, he was raised by his parents' owners and, later graduated with a master's degree in agriculture from Iowa State University, and he filed only three patents even with inventing hundreds of uses of sweet potatoes and peanuts,

"Let us not become weary in doing good, for at the proper time we will reap a harvest if we do not give up" (Galatians 6:9).

"Trust in the LORD with all your heart and lean not on your own understanding; 6 in all your ways submit to him, and he will make your paths straight" (Proverbs 3:5–6).

I may not have personally known Wilma Rudolph, George Washington Carver, or Joseph, but I have encountered special people in my life who had similar experiences and continued to pursue his/her dreams in life in my years of teaching. There have been numerous occasions when there were bushels of lemons thrown in someone's life, yet he/she continued to look up to find the true source of strength, wisdom, and provision. He/She did not allow Satan to dictate his/her standard of life but rather focused on the hope of the salvation of God (i.e., the helmet in the armor of God, the positive expectation of good, the grace, etc.).

We are encountering a new school year with the promise and hope for the future. May we be determined to allow the Lord to make the crooked ways straight as we navigate the turns or hurdles that occur in life. May the excitement of a clean slate, new class, new job, new hobby, new wellness routine, new family, or new career in August be the same at Christmas time or late May when four annual seasons shift.

"I will go before you and make the rough places smooth; I will shatter the doors of bronze and cut through their iron bars" (Isaiah 45:2).

The interesting thing about bronze is that it is inferior to gold or silver. Remember what the temple's external furnishings contained? Bronze. What about the major element of internal furnishings of the temple? Gold. The outside portion of the temple is associated with sacrifices, the atonement for sin. When the word of God states, "I will shatter the doors of bronze," this refers to the performance mind-set of humans—we lean unto our own wisdom rather unto Him. May we rely on Him to crush the enemy, making our path straight and level. Let the Lord go before us. Let Him clear the path. He opens doors that no man may close and shuts doors that no man may open.

"Be strong and courageous. Do not be afraid or terrified because of them, for the LORD your God goes with you; he will never leave you nor forsake you" (Deuteronomy 31:6).

GPA: Honor Child

As I sit in my office, praying about the weekly encouragement, the Lord brings to my mind the struggles I had as a young wife and mother. At the time of my first pregnancy, I had numerous people in my life stressing me out that I needed to do certain things in order to be the best mom, which was to quit work, use organic baby food, use cloth diapers, etc. During that phase of my life, I felt pressured and guilty for not accomplishing all of those particular items, particularly the work and diaper issues. I immediately went down the "condemnation lane" and allowed others to dictate to me the quality of my motherhood based on the quantity of things that I did or did not do or use. Notice I said *quality* and *quantity*. Meanwhile, my son grew and grew in spite of my lack or abundance of actions and love.

Many people think it is either quantitative or qualitative measures to choose, the idea of measuring performance over just love and adoration. Many people get confused about performance and obedience when it pertains to our faith in God. I cannot do enough good things to make God do things in me, through me, or for me. As a Father who loves His kids, He does not keep a record about my performance. My grade point average (GPA) is not a pass or fail grade, but more like a *grace per acceptance.*

Jesus says, "If you have faith as a mustard seed, you will say to this mountain, move from here to there, and it will move; and nothing will be impossible for you" (Matthew 17:20, Luke 17:6). Jesus promises "it will move" (Matthew 17:20), "it will be done" (Matthew 21:21), it "shall come to pass" (Mark 11:23), and it will "obey you" (Luke 17:6).

How much faith did it require? Faith as tiny as a mustard seed. It is not about the quantity; it is about the quality of your faith in God and God's word.

Romans 12:3 says, "For by the grace given to me I say to everyone among you not to think of himself more highly than he ought to think, but to think with sober judgment, each according to the measure of faith that God has assigned."

Faith and unbelief come about as a result of what you hear, read, or believe. The quality of what I focus my attention saturates my hearing and flows out of my mouth and through my actions. Mountains may or may not move depending on my quality of understanding God's word. Do I live in the land of effort, degrees, and titles, or do I live in the land of miraculous potential?

Have you ever thought about why more miracles are reported from desolate areas of the world that have missionaries rather than in our bigger physical structures in the US with its steeples? I have thought about the many missionaries' total reliance on God in those primitive surroundings where he/she cannot rely on anything but the power of God. They have the Word constantly flowing out of their mouths either while reading, praising, or meditating. They are not distracted with man's traditions or advice. It is not the quantity of what they read, sing, or praise, but it is the quality of the time with the Father, praising the author of their faith.

I desire to move, to listen, to obey, to feed on the word of God, to fill my ears with truth from above rather than merely what society dictates as a trend or a solution. I pray for the mountains to be moved out of my life right now whether in relationships, finances, health, or other areas. I desire to be fixated on Christ alone. Praise the Lord for His word, His love, His forgiveness, His grace, and His hope, a confident expectation of good. I am an honored child of God, the highest GPA.

Here's Your Sign!

"**I** cannot believe He told me to build this huge boat and not include any sails. How in the world does the boat maneuver in the water to the destination? Where are we going in this boat? I need to know all of the plans now and not later. Why does the cargo area have to be so big? The construction phase is bringing too many people around my place, asking questions and laughing at me. He tells me that when the boat is complete, the animals are going to show up without me trapping or catching them. My family members need to live on the boat with all of these animals until the water recedes. I am getting nervous about creating this structure in the middle of nowhere, not even close to water. Oh my goodness! What a thunderstorm! The water is rising, and it is getting deeper. Everyone is running toward our boat, screaming. The door is sealed shut. The animals are hibernating within the boat because of the weather. The water is getting deeper outside. We are moving, rocking back and forth with the waves. How long is it going to rain? It seems forever. Help us! Man, the boat reeks of the smells from the animals, the food, etc. I continue to hear the rain pounding on our boat. Now, the intense pounding is fading away. It is beginning to get quiet outside. The animals are beginning to awaken. The water outside the boat is beginning to recede. Now the boat is stopping on this huge mass of land. Where are we now? Oh look, the sun is finally shining. I need to send the dove out one more time to see if the water has receded enough this time. Great, the dove brought back a freshly picked olive leaf in his beak. What is that in the sky? Look at the beautiful colors. What does that mean? I believe you, Lord."

I hope that you recognize the description of Noah in the Book of Genesis. I relate to Noah a great deal, especially during my early years of life when I was making many life/career-type decisions. What is the significance of the rainbow in the sky? It is a clear sign, or promise, that God did not plan to destroy the earth again by water. He offers the rainbow as a sign to Noah. It is a clear picture of the future.

I am such a visual person; I prefer signs or clear directions of what to do in my future. I desire for the rainbows in the sky or maybe a confirmation of what the Holy Spirit is trying to communicate to me. Guess what. In life, we may not get the rainbow to show us the way. How do we know which way to go? We are the ark without sails; we cannot maneuver it to the destination. It is the Holy Spirit that directs us if we are listening. Releasing the ark in the Father's hands is enough for me. I know He loves me. He steers my daily life if I allow Him to do so.

I need to remember the following truths from His word about my life:

"Your word is a lamp for my feet, a light on my path" (Psalm 119:105).

"Trust in the LORD with all your heart and lean not on your own understanding; in all your ways submit to him, and he will make your paths straight" (Proverbs 3:5–6).

"For I know the plans I have for you," declares the LORD, "plans to prosper you and not to harm you, plans to give you hope and a future" (Jeremiah 29:11).

He is my GPS!

"The life of faith is not a life of mounting up with wings, but a life of walking and not fainting... Faith never knows where it is being led, but it loves and knows the One who is leading" (Oswald Chambers).

Horses and Salt Shakers:
Don't Look Back

Due to the summer elementary camp focusing on Texas Parks and Wildlife curriculum, the outdoors, nature, habitats, prey and predators, as well as adaptations, I have been reading more about the unique characteristics of animals. I was fascinated to know more about animals' eyes in comparison to humans. I don't know why lately I am stuck on vision, however, the eyes have it.

Here are a few interesting facts about horses' eyes. Horses have the largest eyes for land mammals; horses use monocular vision since their eyes are set on each side of the head, yet they use binocular vision to focus on things in the distance; horses have 360 degree vision but see things separately rather than together like humans; horses have blind spots directly in front of their heads and behind their tails; horses possess a third eyelid, as well as sensory hairs around the eye to protect it from things while grazing or drinking. This information about horses' vision makes one marvel at the idea of watching horses in competitive equestrian events, jumping hurdles, barrel racing, or other types of events.

The Lord impressed on my heart about the blind spots that horses possess are similar to people's blind spots in life. Sometimes I encounter blind spots in my life, especially whenever I want to go a certain route in my life but cannot see clearly if it is the right way or not. I remembered various times in my life when I wanted to do other things, go in a different direction, and basically went nowhere. It wasn't until, eighteen years ago, a good friend of mine shared with me that if things had to be orchestrated, forced, or made to happen, then it probably was not what the Lord wanted me to do. If things fell into place in an orderly fashion, peacefully without any help from me, then it probably was from the Lord. Bob and I began to use that standard as a red and green light in our lives on what to do.

One of those green lights involved me leaving the classroom with just one class and transitioning to Hardin-Simmons University to be with many future teachers, who would teach their own classes of students. Leaving the classroom eighteen years ago was peaceful and smooth even though I cried a good bit while packing up every-thing. My husband, Bob, was saddened with the instant addition of classroom inventory because I did not get rid of materials, books, and coffee cups because I thought I would use it in my college classes. You know that teachers never throw anything away.

I know the statement about hindsight being 20/20 is quoted often. I don't look back too much of the time because it gets me nowhere in the present. I don't want to be like Lot's wife, wanting to return to something that was not good for me. I joke about keeping a small salt shaker on my desk to remind me to let go of mistakes and move forward after learning from the situation. As a good friend once told Bob and me, "Don't look back!"

I pray[a] that the God of our Lord Jesus, the Messiah,[b] the most glorious Father, would give you a wise spirit, along with revelation that comes through knowing the Messiah[c] fully. Then, with the eyes of your hearts enlightened, you will know the confidence[d] that is produced by God[e] having called you,[f] the rich glory that is his inheritance among the saints, and the unlim-ited greatness of his power for us who believe, according to the working of his mighty strength, which he brought about in the Messiah[g] when he raised him from the dead and seated him at his right hand in the heavenly realm. He is far above every ruler, authority, power, dominion, and every name that can be named, not only in the present age, but also in the one to come.

God[h] has put everything under the Messiah's[i] feet and has made him the head of everything for the good of[j] the church, which is his body, the fullness of the one who fills everything in every way. (James 1:17–23)

"The LORD opens the eyes of the blind; The LORD raises up those who are bowed down; The LORD loves the righteous" (Psalm 146:8).

"And said to him, 'Go, wash in the pool of Siloam' [which is translated, Sent] So he went away and washed, and came back seeing" (John 9:7).

Trusting, obeying, listening, meditating on His word, and walking out my faith, it all reduces the blind spots in my life. The image becomes clearer, unified, and focused. He gently takes the reins of my life and steers me to places He has planned for me in this season of time.

Instead of...

As I reflect about my busy and hectic day, one of the events includes a friend sharing the following verse with me: "Don't fret or worry. *Instead of* worrying, pray. Let petitions and praises shape your worries into prayers, letting God know your concerns. Before you know it, a sense of God's wholeness, everything coming together for good, will come and settle you down. It's wonderful what happens when Christ displaces worry at the center of your life." (Philippians 4:6–7)

The verse solidifies the teaching during our church service tonight—relational thinking. Instead of the glass half empty mind-set (performance thinking), I need the glass half-full mind-set like in relational thinking (realization of who I am in Christ). My mind-set, or what is in the heart, proceeds out of my mouth (Matthew 15:18). Then as I walk out the daily activities of my life, I behave as someone who is in Him and He is in me (John 17:21). When I speak, the words that come out of my mouth please Him (Psalm 19:14), bring life (Proverbs 18:21), and may give grace to those who hear (Ephesians 4:29). My troubles or worries become opportunities to see God's wholeness, everything He is in me. I want to settle down in the blanket of His unrelenting love.

According to the online dictionary, *displacement* means in Freudian psychology (German: Verschiebung, "shift, move") an unconscious defense mechanism whereby the mind substitutes either a new aim or a new object for goals that were felt in their original form to be dangerous or unacceptable.

If I have the mind of Christ (1 Corinthians 2:16), then I possess a new aim or goal that is good, acceptable, and perfect (Romans 12:2) because I am shifting or moving in His direction and not my own. Remember Proverbs 3:5–6 say that lean not unto your own understanding. God has not given me a spirit of fear, but of power, love, and a sound mind (2 Timothy 1:7).

Instead of something, my goal is to replace this part of my daily vocabulary with my birthright as a daughter of Zion. All of His promises are yes and amen. I no longer desire the dangerous or unacceptable mind-set of worrying. God knows my concerns as well as your concerns. He loves you and knows exactly what you are going through right now. Instead of depression, sadness, lack, worry, or dread, come alive in Him.

Interruptions in Life

Courage does not always roar. Sometimes courage is the quiet voice at the end of the day saying, "I will try again tomorrow."
—Mary Anne Radmacher

It is interesting that in any time period of life we have our routines, schedules, or daily plans made and one thing could turn our life upside down. For example, here are a few times I have experienced either a temporary or permanent change in my life:

- Dead battery early in the morning before going to work.
- Blow out of a tire while traveling to TTU from Abilene for my doctoral class (near Hermeleigh of all places)
- A sudden notification that I must move out of a rental or purchase it within thirty days when the owner changed their minds about the long-term goal.
- An offer to be a visiting professor for one year at a university with no assurance for the years that follow while letting go of public school teaching and benefits.
- A sick child in my family in the middle of my school day teaching, ending with a trip to the ER for an appendectomy.
- A sudden phone call to me from back home in Germany, informing me of my dad's death.
- A sudden phone call to me from back home in Abilene, informing me of my mother's death.
- A sudden phone call to us from back home in Biloxi, informing us of Bobby's terrible car accident.

Interruptions in life, Jesus experienced interruptions too. He was busy sharing the good news through stories, healings, discussions with the religious sect, and showing love to those who were unloved, and giving hope to those without hope. People were pressing in and demanding answers, desiring healings, hoping for restoration of relatives' life, expecting royal treatment from a humble servant, or expecting an earthly king to set up shop and rub out all of the enemies immediately. Sometimes He escaped to the mountain or across the sea in a boat.

What about the other people in the Bible who had their lives changed by sudden interruptions?

- Fishermen—Jesus calling them out as disciples
- Zechariah and Elizabeth—angel visiting about John the Baptist
- Mary—angel visiting about Jesus
- Saul—blinding conversion on Damascus road, Paul
- Woman at the well—water of life, Jesus, life changed forever

Interruptions in life, what are you going through right now? How do you perceive it, as an opportunity to learn and grow or as a punishment due to bad luck because of a black cloud following you?

The word of God is truth; it does not change. It is the same yesterday, today, and tomorrow. The Lord loves you. He desires above all things to give you a hope and a future. He does not condemn you. He offers grace and mercy. Take the interruptions as stepping stones to see how God plans to show you more about Him. Look for God's purpose in the next interruption.

> "Trust in the Lord with all your heart, and do not lean on your own understanding. In all your ways acknowledge him, and he will make straight your paths." (Proverbs 3:5–6)

"Now to him who is able to do immeasurably more than all we ask or imagine, according to his power that is at work within us" (Ephesians 3:20).

It's the Journey

My husband, Bob, enjoys picking a random diner or restaurant that he has recently seen on the *Travel Network* and then create a day trip in order to enjoy the cuisine with a few friends or family members. The most recent trip includes traveling to experience Houston's This is It Soul Food in the Houston, Texas area. When I share with other people what Bob is doing, I usually hear things ranging from "That is an expensive meal!" or "Why?" My response is always, "It is not the destination as much as the journey to get there." However, he does love to dine at popular eateries. The journey always contains numerous stories about humorous or shocking things that happen at stops along the way, unusual items on the menu or how full one feels in such a short amount of time. These are just a few things to hear after he returns home. I think Bob could open a travel tour business, A Day's Trip.

My students sometimes feel overwhelmed with the length of time between the freshman year and the actual graduation date. Some of the students think the graduation date may never arrive. The students register each semester to mark off the required courses on their degree plan in order to accomplish the ultimate goal of walking across the stage to receive the diploma. However, a few of the students forget to soak up the learning experiences along the way in order to ensure the successful application of content during job interviews and, ultimately, on teaching positions. The various content and pedagogical courses shape and mold the education majors so they can enter the field of teaching with confidence, plenty of teaching resources from field experiences, and the importance of being a lifelong learner. Each person constantly learns new things along the way.

I think about my walk with the Lord. Sometimes I forget to trust Him during the joyful and the difficult seasons of my life. I want Him to part the waters immediately or move the mountain like Lauren Daigle sings about in her song, "Trust in You." However, I realize the Lord wants me to trust Him more as I travel along the way. I need to appropriate all of my inheritance before the great beyond. It is the process, the journey rather than the destination.

In Deuteronomy 31:6, I read, "Be strong and courageous. Do not fear or be in dread of them, for it is the Lord your God who goes with you. He will not leave you or forsake you."

I notice in the verse, "Lord your God who goes with you." *Goes* is a present tense verb. He is with me on my journey whether I recognize Him or not. I guess it gives proof to the verse in Exodus 3:14: "God said to Moses, 'I AM WHO I AM. This is what you are to say to the Israelites: "I AM has sent me to you."'" He is currently right here with me in my storm or sunshine season of life. He knows exactly where I am, and He promises to give *joy and peace* within all seasons (Romans 15:13). The journey is where He molds and teaches me His ways, His precepts, His truth. It is not just something I memorize in my mind, but it becomes a way of life each day.

I know that in teaching, we always talk about how the process is so important rather than focusing on the product at the end or focusing on a test score. As a teacher, I want to know the mental processes the students go through to arrive at the solution or final product. I want to see if there are any gaps, any bits of information needed in order to refine or reteach, etc. The process or journey determines the ease or smoothness in accomplishing the task or goal. The learners trust the teacher to prepare opportunities for success. I trust the Lord! Jeremiah 29:11 says, "'For I know the plans I have for you,' declares the LORD, 'plans to prosper you and not to harm you, plans to give you hope and a future.'"

His plans are higher than mine. His ways are much better than my ways (Isaiah 55:9). "To You, O Lord, I lift up my soul. O my God, I trust in you… Show me your ways, O Lord; Teach me your paths. Lead me in your truth and teach me, for you are the God of my salvation; On You I wait all the day" (Psalm 25:1–5).

Through a few e-mails today, a good friend and colleague reminds me of one of my dad's favorite songs, "Farther Along." I realize Brad Paisley's version is probably the popular choice to play, but my memories include playing the piano while Dad sits beside me with his harmonica joining in at different times. This is part of the refrain:

Farther along we'll know all about it, farther along we'll understand why. Cheer up my brother, live in the sunshine, We'll understand it all by and by.

The total understanding is the destination; the journey is my process in understanding how to live each day trusting in the Lord. I need the *Son to shine* as I go through all seasons of my journey.

Knock, Knock, Who's There?

I decided to highlight an *obscure* person who believed in the power of prayer and spreading the news. It is a female teenage servant named Rhoda. As I researched the story about Rhoda, I noticed a website listing a few fictional and historical figures named Rhoda. I wanted to remind you of a few of these females.

a. Rhoda Morgenstern (Valerie Harper) (1970–74) is Mary Tyler Moore's best friend and upstairs neighbor. (Maybe you have seen the sitcom show on *Nick at Night.*)

b. Rhoda Montemayor (born 1979), an actress who played Rose Ortiz, the Pink Ranger in *Power Rangers: Operation Overdrive.*

c. Rhoda Abbott (1873–1946), the only female passenger to go down with the *Titanic* and survive.

d. Rhoda Scott (born 1938), an African American hard bop and soul jazz organist.

e. Rhoda Richards (1784–1879), the wife of Mormon leader Joseph Smith and, after his death, Brigham Young.

Rhoda in the Bible

An individual mentioned once in the New Testament, appears only in Acts 12:12–15. She left Peter standing at the door after he was miraculously released from prison. Prayers were immediately answered. She was so overjoyed. She rushed to tell the news and left him outside the door. After she shared the news with the group of friends (prayer partners), who had just finished praying for Peter's release, they told Rhoda that it was probably Peter's angel. Peter continued to knock on the door. Finally, they all heard him knocking and greeted him with joy. Just imagine how relieved Peter was; he knew the soldiers would be looking for him.

Rhoda was the servant of Mary, the mother of Mark. The Greek name, Rhoda, means *rose,* which offers a sweet fragrance. Rhoda served the family all hours of the day and night. Peter arrived at the house very late. Paul described Rhoda's immediate response of joy and the recognition of Peter's voice, which meant an answer to prayer. Just think about it, a door separated the people praying for something and the answer to that prayer (John 10:9: "I am the door. If anyone enters by Me, he will be saved, and will go in and out and find pasture"). All the while, a servant was the messenger (Matthew 20:28: "Just as the Son of Man did not come to be served, but to serve, and to give his life as a ransom for many").

Rhoda forgot about her position as a servant, she just ran in excitement to tell the good news that Peter was out of prison. Even when the group belittled her message, she stood her ground. She believed in the Word that she had heard earlier. She continued to tell the good news. Finally, the others heard the knocking and Peter's voice, and they opened the door (Mark 16:15: "And then he told them, "Go into all the world and preach the Good News to everyone").

Here were a few things that stood out to me as I read about Rhoda:

- Jesus is not a respecter of persons, no matter your status, titles, position, wealth, etc. (Romans 2:11 "For God does not show favoritism.")
- Praise and gratitude bring a sweet aroma over the world (2 Corinthians 2:14: "But thank God! He has made us his captives and continues to lead us along in Christ's triumphal procession. Now he uses us to spread the knowledge of Christ everywhere, like a sweet perfume.")
- What you personally hear matters. Do not depend on the other voices. (Deuteronomy 31:6: "Be strong and courageous. Do not be afraid or terrified because of them, for the LORD your God goes with you; he will never leave you nor forsake you.")

- Prayers are answered (1 John 5:14–15: "And this is the confidence that we have toward him, that if we ask anything according to his will he hears us. And if we know that he hears us in whatever we ask, we know that we have the requests that we have asked of him").

Remember Rhoda, serving, sharing, praising, and standing on the word. Do not grow weary in doing good (Galatians 6:9).

Lions, Tigers, and Bears... Oh My!

Last weekend, my two daughters and their families visited the Abilene Zoo. As they walked around the exhibits, they paused at the cougar site. The two cougars were sleeping comfortably in their fabricated habitat, which was completely enclosed. Somehow, a bird happened to squeeze through an opening that led him or her into the private domain of these lean, wild felines. As the bird flew about the exhibit, the cougars were startled with the sudden "fast food" possibility, they immediately remembered their native trapping skills. All three of my grandchildren (ages nine, four, and two) watched the cougars chase and then slowly stalk the bird. From my daughter's brief video, it was almost like watching the Discovery Channel or *Animal Kingdom*. The bird panicked while trying to retrace its steps (or flaps) to escape this unending chase. Unfortunately, the bird flew to a low branch on the ground; one cougar pounced and feathers flew everywhere. Immediately, my four-year-old granddaughter began to cry. The remaining family members observed the cougar's entire dining experience. My granddaughter retold the story numerous times, saying, "The mean tigers ate the bird."

Prey, predators, chasing, pouncing, and ultimately death. I have been thinking about how I have fallen into enclosed habitats, offices, classes, or family dwellings and allowed the enemy to frighten me or cause me to panic. It has never been any physical bullying, but more like mental or emotional attacks. Then I remembered this verse, Ephesians 6:12: "For our struggle is not against flesh and blood, but against the rulers, against the authorities, against the powers of this dark world and against the spiritual forces of evil in the heavenly realms."

Think about Daniel in the lions' den. Go back and reread the beginning chapters of the Book of Daniel. Remember that due to Daniel's eating plan or fast, his wisdom was unmatched by others surrounding the king. You have to know that Daniel had made quite a few enemies who wanted to be the king's advisors, the ones who wanted to sit on the king's right side at the table, etc. These "cougars" observed Daniel's every move. When he refused to compromise his beliefs, these "roaring lions" or observers pounced. Daniel ended up in the lions' den.

"A stone was brought and placed over the mouth of the den, and the king sealed it with his own signet ring and with the rings of his nobles, so that Daniel's situation might not be changed" (Daniel 6:17).

When the outside world sees my situation, they view it as a done deal. No escape. I must suffer from the enemy's lies, accusations, or fear. However, the inside world (the spirit world) views the real king, and knows His verdict is "it is finished. He shut the mouths of the lions! No more pain, no more suffering. He is my advocate. He loves me, and I am free of any condemnation." The stone has been rolled away.

Fast forward to the end of Daniel's story after the king releases him from the den; no wound was found on him. His enemies were crushed by the same lions in the den, and Daniel prospered.

"Peace I leave with you; my peace I give you. I do not give to you as the world gives. Do not let your hearts be troubled and do not be afraid" (John 14:27).

"We have an advocate with the Father, Jesus Christ the righteous" (1 John 2:1).

Do not bow down to anything other than the Lord Almighty. He is your advocate, defender, and healer. Renew your mind daily, feed on the Word rather than others' accusations and focus on the empty tomb, the stone has been rolled away!

Live Long and Prosper

The past few weeks, I have been focusing on major life events or on people—Mother's Day, graduation, weddings, anniversaries, jobs/careers, etc. So many seasons for different people who I care about or love.

A few seasons of time seem to take forever while a weekend or even the summer seems to fly by. We have an ongoing joke with some friends that on July 4 we call each other and wish them a Merry Christmas. We have laughed about how time flies by from the summer to the winter holidays. Ye, when we were young children or teenagers, time dragged by. Where do you seem to be right now? Is time dragging or flying by?

What does the Word say about time?

"But do not overlook this one fact, beloved, that with the Lord one day is as a thousand years, and a thousand years as one day" (2 Peter 3:8).

"Jesus Christ is the same yesterday and today and forever" (Hebrews 13:8).

"Set your minds on things that are above, not on things that are on earth" (Colossians 3:2).

Okay, so instead of setting our clocks forward or backward, we need to set our minds on things that are above. What are those things? I need to be reminded if He is the same yesterday, today, and forever. If I am truly a citizen of the kingdom of God, then my language matches it because my mind is fixed on those things my father does or believes. If I have a renewed mind, then my thoughts are about things that are permanent and not temporary or trendy on earth. I need to be the same as He is. As He is, so am I. I am not focused on the amount of time, the season of time, or the past. I am living each day with a grateful heart for the seasons the Lord has provided grace so I can endure or thrive. With Him, all things are possible. I can do all things through Christ, who strengthens me.

Tonight in our church group, someone mentioned the Spock saying with the V hand gesture, "Live long and prosper" on *Star Trek*. Bob explained the Leonard Nimoy's Jewish background and the reason for the saying. It was a blessing. The gesture makes the Hebrew letter, *shin*, which is the first letter in several words: *Shaddai (God)*, *shalom*, *Shekhinah*. It reminds one of the Aaronic Blessing in Numbers 6:24–27:

The Lord bless you
and keep you;
the Lord make his face shine on you
and be gracious to you;
the Lord turn his face toward you
and give you peace.

LOL: OMG Reigns!

When I was a kid, one of my favorite things about going on a trip with my family was the time I spend with my dad. Yes, I was guilty of asking questions like "Are we there yet?" but I loved to hear my dad sing or tell funny stories along the way. I have decided that if he had completed a multiple intelligence inventory, he probably would have scored highest in the linguistic portion. He made up goofy stories that included figures of speech as punch lines. One of my favorite stories that he shared was the following (he always told the story quickly while having fun with the words):

> Once upon a time, there was a family of skunks who lived in the woods. The mother skunk named the two baby skunks, In and Out. When In was in, Out was out. When In was out, Out was in the house. One day, the mother skunk called both baby skunks in for dinner. Out came in, but In did not. The mother skunk asked Out to go out to find In and bring In in the house. So Out went out to find In and bring him home. A few hours later, Out brought In in the house. The mother skunk was so happy and relieved. She asked Out how did he find In to bring In in so quickly. Out said, "Easy. In stinks!"

Do not worry for fear of other stories. I hope that you chuckled or found a bit of humor in the short skunk tale (Ha, just a bit more of my corny humor). My intention was to bring a bit of humor in a busy time of the semester or season of life. This week's happy Thursday is light-hearted but hopefully encouraging.

> Laughter is poison to fear.
>
> —George R.R. Martin

Yesterday, a good friend of ours from Florida visited briefly with a few members of my family. We were catching up with each other's lives over dinner at one of our favorite restaurants. We chatted about various topics. One of the questions that he asked one of my children, who was eating with us, was "What makes you laugh?" It was a funny question but yet so deep. I began to think about myself. What made me laugh?

Immediately, I thought I about all of the pranks that I pulled on family and friends along the way, both young and older, I then mentally replayed a few funny videos on Facebook and the scary episodes of snakes or spiders on the magic show, *The Carbonera Effect*. Lately, I have laughed a good bit at my children and grandchildren, retelling mispronounced words, or those embarrassing things that happen in line at the store, or the clever reasons about not wanting to go to bed at night. I have laughed a good bit at Bob, sharing his adventures this past Christmas with his parents who visited us for twelve days.

> I don't trust anyone who doesn't laugh.
>
> —Maya Angelou

I have been around plenty of people who refuse to smile or laugh. The glass is always half empty, no joy whatsoever. The "woe is me" look drapes on the face to cover any sign of hope or gratitude. If someone views only the negative in life and does not see any silver lining on the clouds, the narrative rehearsed includes lies from the enemy. I am not saying to laugh all of the time. Life is difficult sometimes. The Lord does not promise us a life without storms. However, He does provide peace within the storms.

"Then our mouths were filled with laughter and our tongues with joyful songs. Then the nations said, "The LORD has done spectacular things for them." The LORD has done spectacular things for us. We are overjoyed" (Psalm 126:2–3).

"Then he said to them, 'Go, eat of the fat, drink of the sweet, and send portions to him who has nothing prepared; for this day is holy to our Lord. Do not be grieved, *for the joy of the LORD is your strength*" (Nehemiah 8:10).

"In a little while, the world will see Me no more, but you will see Me. Because I live, you also will live. On that day you will know that I am in My Father, and you are in Me, and I am in you" (John 14:19–20).

"I have no greater joy than to hear that my children are walking in the truth" (3 John 1:4).

What's the Manna with You?

I cannot imagine waking in the morning and walking outside to find food provided from heaven for my day – white flakes that taste like thin cakes made with honey. Just imagine you and your friends in the desert wandering around without food. The Lord tells you about the food that He plans to rain down on you as long as the sun is up each day. When the sun sets, the food melts away. You are not allowed to save any for the next day. It is just enough for one day. This makes the Paleo-diet, Trim Healthy Mama plan, or Atkins menus seem like a feast. However, the flakes, or manna, is just enough for you for the day. He loves you. Read Exodus 16:1–36.

What is your day like? What types of things are you enduring right now? Are you lacking energy, clear mind, joy, finances, confidence, contentment, or rest? Do you feel like you are in an intense desert experience right now feeling weak and hopeless? Are you feeling like you are dehydrated, not of physical food or water, but of peace, wisdom, or direction about something? Guess what.

> The steps of a man are established by the Lord,
> And He delights in his way.
> Though he falls, he will not be hurled headlong,
> Because the Lord is the One who holds his hand.
> (Psalm 37:23–24)

I love how David reflects about his own life – the good, the bad, and the ugly times in his youth. He thinks about the times of need. Notice he states "the steps of a man." Steps involve short distances, not a mile or even a marathon. It is the right now of your journey. Which way are you going? *Established* conveys bringing about or into existence. You do not have to come up with the solution: you seek His ways, His direction, and His provision. Do not lean unto your own understanding. The next part of the scripture is "though he falls," not if but when. We are humans; we sometimes stumble financially, emotionally, or maybe spiritually.

"A man's mind plans his way, but the Lord directs his steps and makes them sure" (Proverbs 16:9).

"To open doors before him so that gates will not be shut: I will go before you and make the rough places smooth; I will shatter the doors of bronze and cut through their iron bars. I will give you the treasures of darkness And hidden wealth of secret places, So that you may know that it is I, The LORD, the God of Israel, who calls you by your name" (Isaiah 45:1–3).

The last part of Psalm 37:24 mentions the Lord is the "One who holds his hand" (or your hand). You are not alone right now. The powerful creator of the heavens and the earth, who spoke things into existence, who knew you before you were born, who has your steps ordered holds your hand. What a feeling of security. He is like the dad catching the son who is falling from a tree limb, grabbing his daughter's arm to prevent her from entering the busy street, guiding the toddler to walk for the first time from one parent to another, or hugging the child after waking up from a nightmare. No matter the situation, He is holding your hand through the situation. He is providing the manna you need for such a time as this. *Mangia!* (Italian for "to eat.") Taste and see that the Lord is good (Psalm 34:8).

Melt Your Worries Away

Believe it or not, I had a high school teacher who spoke to me after class about being worried and stressed. He said, "Renee, you are way too serious about your schoolwork." I realize that it seems like he would want me to be serious about my schoolwork, but he realized I was exhibiting signs of anxiety and burnout. Little did he know that I placed pressure on myself because I needed to do extra things in order to retain the information. I was not dyslexic; however, I did process information in a different way. I learned more in a visual and hands-on way, which most teachers did not use in my junior high or high school classes. It was a "one size fits all" mentality of teaching and learning, which did not fit me.

"I tell you not to worry about your life. Don't worry about having something to eat, drink or wear. Isn't life more important than food or clothing? Look at the birds in the sky! They don't plant or harvest. They don't even store grain in barns. Yet your Father in heaven takes care of them. Aren't you worth more than birds. Can worry make you live longer?" (Matthew 6:25–27).

Isn't it amazing that over 70 percent of the American population have some form of stress, whether physical or psychological according to Stress Statistics. We tend to want to make things go away or just fix it, which is all about the symptoms rather than the cause. Stress consumes the whole body—emotions, physical health, social responses, as well as spiritual contentment. Our minds become overwhelmed with the external stressors, and we lose focus on the God of peace.

Overwhelmed, according to the online dictionary:

- to overpower or overcome, especially with superior forces; destroy; crush
- to cover or bury beneath a mass of something, as floodwaters, debris, or an avalanche; submerge
- to load, heap, treat, or address with an overpowering or excessive amount of anything

If I asked any undergraduate or graduate student right now how things are, the majority of the students will respond with a feeling of being overwhelmed. If I asked colleagues or friends outside the university world, the answer may be the same due to the hurriedness of life, the approaching holidays, the end of the first semester of the school year, family/health issues, etc. I sense a crushing atmosphere from all around us, things bombarding our minds and hearts to rob us of the peace that we have within us. We have choices to make each day.

I wonder sometimes what life was like for those early Christians living in Jerusalem or in nearby communities. Did the commerce workers or religious people get so busy, they felt overwhelmed? Did they worry about numerous things related to family dynamics, health issues, education, religion, politics, and economics? *Yes,* they did. Here are just a few of the verses spoken to different groups of people during this time period as well as to us.

"Peace I leave with you; my peace I give you. I do not give to you as the world gives. Do not let your hearts be troubled and do not be afraid" (John 14:27).

"Commit to the LORD whatever you do, and he will establish your plans" (Proverbs 16:3).

"I have commanded you to be strong and brave. Don't ever be afraid or discouraged! I am the Lord your God, and I will be there to help you wherever you go" (Joshua 1:9).

"I sought the Lord, and he answered me and delivered me from all my fears" (Psalm 34:4).

Stress cannot exist in an atmosphere of praise, joy, peace, and strength. Through a commitment to the Lord for my daily plans, wisdom and direction follow. I make wise decisions about priorities, about the big and small matters of my life, as well as distinguishing things that are urgent or important in my life. I desire peace today and tomorrow, as well as the years to come. Praise the Lord for He is good all of the time. His mercies are new every morning. He does not let me down. He loves me just like He loves you.

Nearsightedness: Visual Acuity

"Dear Lord, thank you for our food and water. Please bless Brady and my friend, Brandon. Thank you for my family. Give us safe travels. Bless the homeless and keep them safe. Bless my mommy, BeBob and Nay Nay, Aunt Shannon, Uncle Jeremy, Shelby, Marcus, Uncle Bobby, Aunt Anna, Robert and Killian. Thank you for our food and water. Please make Rachel's grandfather well. And thank you for your *greatness*. In Jesus's name. Amen."

This is a nightly routine that I am blessed to be a part of with my grandson, Brody. Each time he talks to God, he asks certain blessings over family and friends as well as express his gratitude for big and small blessings. What a lesson of innocence. However, tonight his appreciation for the Lord's greatness struck me in a powerful way.

Greatness:

- unusual or considerable in degree, power, intensity, etc. (online dictionary)
- remarkable or outstanding in magnitude, degree, or extent (*The Free Dictionary*)

"Great is the LORD and most worthy of praise; his greatness no one can fathom. They tell of the power of your awesome works and I will proclaim your great deeds" (Psalm 145:3 and 6).

Childlike faith—to view the creator of the universe and all of the inhabitants, the author and finisher, the beginning and the end and see His greatness. Today, my vision has not been 20/20. I have allowed external influences or distractions to cloud my perspective.

I am not an expert on this topic like a good friend of ours in San Antonio is. However, curiosity caused me to research about vision for a brief time. Visual acuity means the clarity or sharpness of vision. This does not mean perfect vision. According to an online source, visual acuity also involves peripheral awareness or side vision, eye coordination, depth perception, focusing ability, and color vision, all of which contributes to an overall visual ability. Others can see items that are close but cannot see those far away. This condition may be caused by myopia (nearsightedness). In this sense, I think Brody has the ability to see beyond the immediate circumstances, whether social, financial, emotional, or physical. His visual acuity stretches across the horizon to praise the Lord for His unusual *power, intensity, magnitude,* and *love.* Way to go, Brody. I pray you never lose your ability to see beyond the immediate.

"For now we see in a mirror dimly, but then face to face; now I know in part, but then I will know fully just as I also have been fully known" (1 Corinthians 13:12).

"Now faith is the assurance of things hoped for, the conviction of things not seen" (Hebrews 11:1).

I could eat leafy vegetables, egg yolks, berries, almonds, and fatty fish for healthy eyes. However, my spiritual vision comes from reviewing the word of God, repeating the testimony of His goodness, renewing my mind on promises from God, and thinking on things that are pure, true, whatever is noble, whatever is right, whatever is pure, whatever is lovely, whatever is admirable. If anything is excellent or praiseworthy, think about such things.

Thank you, Lord, for my prayer times with Brody.

No Dress Rehearsal:
The Real Deal

Several things are happening this week: Teacher Appreciation Week, honoring fallen officers, final exams and graduation, and Mother's Day. Talk about a rollercoaster of emotions. I am overwhelmed with by seeing many chapters of life ending and beginning. I enjoy reading all the postings on Facebook about our HSU alumni ending another year of teaching, counting down the days, as well as sharing the hand-written notes of appreciation from their students. I also am grateful for the kind cards, e-mails, and Facebook postings from my current students and "soon to be" graduates (i.e., undergraduate students, doctoral students, graduate students completing a master in education while others are completing certificate requirements) who are also counting how many finals remain before the summer break or "adulting" begins. My heart breaks as I reflect on the many fallen law enforcement officers nationwide as well as locally. I pray for Adam Ybarra and his daughter, Noelle, the Police Detective Christopher Milliorn; and my son, Bobby, as they reflect about the life and career of Elise ending so quickly last August. Finally, my heart is full of love and gratitude as I reflect on my mother, as well as the blessing of my husband, three children and their families. It is amazing how my children are now parents, receiving the handmade cards and hugs from their little ones. The time you are currently living in, whether as a student, a teacher, a business person, an administrator, a retired government employee, or one transitioning into a new career may last a month, a year, or the remainder of your life. God is faithful and gracious to all of us, no matter the season of time, whether chaotic, peaceful, disappointing, exciting, overwhelming, or fulfilling. He is the first and the last, the beginning and the end (Isaiah 48:12).

"And, in the beginning, Lord, you laid the foundation of the earth, and the heavens are the work of your hands" (Hebrews 1:10).

"To everything there is a season, and a time to every purpose under the heaven" (Ecclesiastes 3:1).

I remember writing a short poem about my favorite principal, who hired me when we moved to Abilene, Mr. Sam Thomas. He was an amazing educator, friend, husband, and dad. I was saddened when he passed away during my second year of working for him. He was a unique administrator, teacher, and leader. He had a unique way of making everyone feel special and loved. While he was in the hospital, I visited Mr. Thomas and his wife. I read the poem to him and left it with his wife when I departed. I wanted him to hear how much he meant to me. Mrs. Thomas saved it and gave it to our PTA later for the special memorial ceremony which consisted of the students and teachers singing and sharing about their memories of Mr. Thomas, along with representatives from the district/campus planting a tree in his honor. The PTA placed a brick memorial with a plaque at the base of the tree trunk. My poem was engraved on the plaque. They asked me to read the poem at the ceremony. Later, I jokingly said that I was published in stone. Here is the poem that I wrote about Mr. Thomas:

One Man's Life

Seconds of direction and advice
Minutes of jokes and laughter
Hours of sharing and encouraging
Days of tenderness and compassion
Weeks of leading and teaching
Months of strength and endurance
Years of knowledge and wisdom –
A LIFETIME OF LOVE!

Mr. Thomas believed that each day was a turning point for someone in our sphere of influence. He encouraged the teachers and staff members to make each moment count for all the students on the campus. He reminded all of us that our words and our actions spoke volumes to the people around us. He desired that our campus be a place to encourage dreams, careers, and hope. Anyone who knew and loved Mr. Thomas felt like they could jump over skyscrapers because of his belief in us.

Guess what? God believes in us too. He does not think it, but He knows that we have the same power within us through Christ Jesus to do the things that are impossible to many people. He desires that His children realize that each day of our lives is full of opportunities to demonstrate His love, joy, peace, forgiveness, and justice. Your decisions today influence the future. Celebrate your family and friends now rather than later. Do everything as unto the Lord (Colossians 3:23).

Make each day count. Those days evolve into weeks, months, years, and a lifetime.

No Fear: Bases Loaded
with Two Strikes

According to an online source, KidsHealth.org, the top five fears of children are

- scary movies and TV shows;
- nightmares and scary dreams;
- thunderstorms, hurricanes, and other violent weather;
- war and terrorism; and
- sounds I hear at night.

According to data taken from Google, the top five fears of adults are

- flying,
- public speaking,
- heights,
- dark, and
- intimacy.

Fear is defined as "an unpleasant feeling of apprehension or distress caused by the presence or anticipation of danger." I heard a pastor share about the word FEAR (false evidence appearing real).

The first fear mentioned in the Bible involved Adam when he hid from God in the garden. Much later, after Moses sent out the twelve spies, ten returned, clamoring about the giants in the land and forfeited the promise of God. Another example of fear involved Jonah not wanting to preach to the people of Nineveh. In the New

Testament, the rich young ruler was afraid to give up his lifestyle to follow Jesus.

Think of the heroes mentioned in the Hebrew 11's hall of fame: the person who built an ark, brought the walls of Jericho down, stopped the mouths of the lions, quenched the raging fire, and even raised the dead. They were ordinary people who allowed the word of God to supersede the emotions felt at the time: no fear because of the love of God. Each person pressed forward in spite of what he/she saw with their physical eyes, heard with their ears, or touched with their hands.

"For the Spirit God gave us does not make us timid, but gives us power, love and self-discipline" (2 Timothy 1:7).

"There is no fear in love. But perfect love drives out fear, because fear has to do with punishment. The one who fears is not made perfect in love" (1 John 4:18).

What about current times? Everyone has a tendency to stay in the comfort of their own lives, not venturing out into the unknown, afraid of the ifs, and the anticipation of danger. Sometimes peer pressure is worse as an adult than when we were younger. What if the teacher next door dislikes my teaching style? What if the supervisor disagrees with my view of honesty with customers? What if I cannot pursue my parents' views of a successful career? What if I let go of my classroom and teach at the university? What if? Just fill in the blanks.

Who is the author and finisher of your faith? Who is the source of your strength, you or the Lord? What is your source of strength, power, and sound mind? Is it vitamins, essential oils, degree, or the latest best-selling book? Are you leaning unto your own understanding? Follow the peace in your heart. If you have to make things happen, do not go in that direction. If things fall into your lap with ease and you have peace from the Lord about it, run in that direction. Follow His ways. Run home to Him! He has plans to prosper you and give you a hope and a future.

Overwhelm Me

I do not know about you, but every now and then, I feel as if I am quickly moving through a long and winding maze, frantically searching for a way out. The surrounding walls seems to shrink around me, choking the life out of me as I turn every corner. However, I pursue the end of the tunnel, looking for an escape from some people and things around me. I do not know why I allow the enemy to trap me like this periodically, but I sometimes forget the path the Lord has for me, Proverbs 3:5 says, "In all your ways acknowledge Him, And He will make your paths straight." I allow my five senses to dictate my perceived realities with no escape. Tunnel vision prohibits the full kingdom vision, which is to walk as a victor not a victim, to take every step knowing that He loves me and cares for me, and to own and live out my inheritance from Him.

I sometimes ponder about the disciples hanging out with Jesus and listening to His teachings like cursing a fig tree, spitting in the dirt to heal a blind man, using wheat as a part of his lessons, casting a net on one side of the boat to catch fish, or allowing the woman to use perfume to wash his feet. Then as Jesus explains that He is leaving but not to worry because there is an advocate, a helper, or companion coming who does only what the Father says to do (John 5:19). The disciples feel a bit of panic and cry out for Jesus to stay with them. He exudes power, love, safety, peace and a perceived reality. The disciples feel a bit of anxiousness, not knowing what to expect, but Jesus promises He is leaving them peace (John 16). I imagine the maze of life feeling entering a few of their hearts and minds. The walls are closing in tightly squeezing out the amount of faith they really possess.

The mazes in my life seem overwhelming sometimes. However, the word of the Lord offers this truth in 2 Corinthians 4:17: "For our light and momentary troubles are achieving for us an eternal glory that far outweighs them all. I Peter 5:10 In his kindness God called you to share in his eternal glory by means of Christ Jesus. So after you have suffered a little while, he will restore, support, and strengthen you, and he will place you on a firm foundation."

He restores, supports, strengthens me and then places me on a firm foundation. I love the images of restoration: "He restores the joy of my salvation" (Psalm 52:12), "He restores my health" (Jeremiah 30:17), "He restores the fortune or financial things robbed by the enemy" (Job 42:10), "He restores a double portion of honor for any shame. Then I think about how He strengthens me" (Isaiah 61:7), "It is through hope in the Lord" (Isaiah 40:31), "The joy of the Lord is my strength" (Nehemiah 8:10), "When I don't know how to pray in my weakness, the Spirit intercedes for me" (Romans 8:26), and "The Lord's power is made perfect in my weakness...when I am weak He makes me strong" (2 Corinthians. 12:9–10).

"Each time he said, 'My grace is all you need. 'My power works best in weakness.' So now I am glad to boast about my weaknesses, so that the power of Christ can work through me" (2 Corinthians 12:9).

Paradox: The Lion and the Lamb

As I travel each day to teach at Hardin-Simmons University, I listen to either songs or messages to help me focus for the day. Today's topic from Graham Cooke includes the issue of paradoxes in a Christian's life. We know the first shall be last, it is better to give than receive, beauty for ashes, and in order to lead one must be a servant. Jesus did enjoy using the foolish things to confound the wise. It is simple yet complex.

"That is why, for Christ's sake, I delight in weaknesses, in insults, in hardships, in persecutions, in difficulties. For when I am weak, then I am strong" (2 Corinthians 12:10).

A *paradox* is something (such as a situation) that is made up of two opposite things and that seems impossible but is actually true or possible (*Merriam-Webster* online).

This Thursday message is very short. I know I am not alone in this stage of life right now, gaining strength through hardships. Many of you who read this weekly e-mail could share about your own experiences and how the Lord made you stronger. A good friend loves to share one of her favorite verses during a similar time of life. In fact, she is an inspiration to me due to her joyful testimony to God's goodness during the losses of family members and sickness over two years.

"And provide for those who grieve in Zion—to bestow on them a crown of beauty instead of ashes, the oil of joy instead of mourning, and a garment of praise instead of a spirit of despair. They will be called oaks of righteousness, a planting of the LORD for the display of his splendor" (Isaiah 61:3).

He is my defender. He is my shield. He makes all things right in the middle of when all things are going wrong.

Position Yourself for a Blessing

This week's e-mail may be one of the briefest messages of encouragement due to a trip across the southeast. After listening to several rich encouraging messages recently, I want to send each of you a message of refreshment and encouragement.

Rather than focusing on the unknown future—whether this is a new semester in school, a new job or career, or a new relationship, or just a new year—focus on the planner; the designer; the matchmaker; the curriculum director; the Son of the living God, Jesus. In this time of year, I send cards with creative manger scenes, as well as the midnight sky with the illuminating light of the star. I attend the beautifully orchestrated and rehearsed programs to reflect the many songs and characters popular for the season. I read the many biblical accounts of the Christmas story in my Bible. I give thanks for His birth, His death, and His resurrection. All to say, I know logically the reason for the season. However, do I really know the reason for my life on this earth? What does the future hold for me? I pray for wisdom about the future. I pray for the many people I love and care about. I pray for the strangers, who I don't know but care about what happens to them. I begin to feel twinges of fear and doubt creep slowly into my renewed mind each day. I don't know about you, but sometimes, I allow the doubt and fear to become like a snowball rolling down a mountain. Pretty soon, the snowball is an avalanche of defeat, confusion, and complications. I rise again, shaking the snow off of myself and look up to find my help. How much time do I waste doing this each year? I need to live 365 days, 24/7 with the renewed mind of Christ. If I do, all of my prayers line up with His will, I then see a change in my life.

According to Mark Batterson *(Mark Batterson, The Circle Maker: Praying Circles Around Your Biggest Dreams and Greatest Fears* [Grand Rapids, MI: Zondervan, 2016], 54), "When you live in obedience, you position yourself for blessing. And you never know how or when or where God is going to show up."

I plan to seek Him first and lean not unto my own understanding. I look forward to 2017 and the many blessings that He has with my name on it. What about you? Pray to seek His opportunities, His mate, His job, His GPA, etc. He loves to bless His children. You and I are His children.

Prisoner of Hope

Picture a young man about sixteen years old, wanting to join the navy to be with his older brother, who had just deployed to the Pacific region. This sixteen-year-old, Jimmy, changed his birthdate on the birth certificate to ensure his enlistment. Jimmy became a Frogman, someone trained in scuba diving or swimming underwater in a tactical capacity. Since Jimmy was from a small Georgia community, Milledgeville, he pictured that he would immediately be side by side with his brother, Walter. Little did Jimmy know that he would meet up with Walter at Pearl Harbor prior to December 7, 1941. After the attack on Pearl Harbor, Walter and Jimmy never saw one another until after the war was over, and they returned to the United States. During Jimmy's time in the Pacific, he lost a kneecap in one excursion, an eardrum in an underwater explosion, and played dead underneath dead American soldiers on the beach of one of the islands; he was stabbed with a bayonet through his spleen as a lookout squad came through the beach, looking for Americans who survived. Later, he was captured and became a prisoner of war for a while on one of the islands. Jimmy suffered physical and mental anguish during that time. For example, he endured sharpened bamboo sticks under his fingernails until the ultimate removal of the nails from the hands. When he repeated the oath to defend and support the Constitution of the United States, Jimmy had no idea of all that was ahead of him for the next twenty-six years of service to the United States. Jimmy survived WWII, the Korean conflict, and Vietnam. He retired in 1967 as a Senior Master Sergeant in the United States Air Force. Many saluted him as SMSgt. Brown on military installations, but at home, he was my dad, James R. Brown (yes, James Brown).

"Return to the stronghold, O prisoners who have the hope; This very day I am declaring that I will restore double to you" (Zechariah 9:12).

As I walk through life, I am aware of the tribulations that bombard my life from different events or phases of time. I think about the mountaintop experiences as well as the valleys that I have traveled in my life. The journey reminds me of the Stockdale paradox, named after Admiral Jim Stockdale, who was a prisoner of war during the Vietnam War. He explains the paradox as confronting the brutal facts or the reality of life but never losing your faith. The paradox embraces the hope of the future while dealing day to day with the events that come across your path. It is more about how confident you are in knowing the end of the story rather than the current chapter you are living out today.

I am a prisoner of hope. Hope means a confident expectation of good. In one of Mark Batterson's sermons, he shares that love is our calling card, our faith is like a credit card while hope is a greeting card. It conveys wishes for the future. As a Christian, it is not about wishes. It is about truth or a reality, not like the world knows or understands. Hope is who we are because of God's glory.

"Through him we have also obtained access by faith into this grace by which we have been established, and we boast because of our hope in God's glory. Not only that, but we also boast in our sufferings, knowing that suffering produces endurance, endurance produces character, and character produces hope. Now this hope does not disappoint us, because God's love has been poured out into our hearts by the Holy Spirit, who has been given to us" (Romans 5:2–5).

Just think about this: you are free to be a prisoner of hope.

Rat Race versus His Race

Hebrews 12:1 says, "Therefore, since we are surrounded by such a great cloud of witnesses, let us throw off everything that hinders and the sin that so easily entangles. And let us run with perseverance the race marked out for us."

This verse is a strong part of my life right now. Here are some personal thoughts about the verse. Hope it blesses you.

- I love the image of a *group of witnesses* surrounding me. Think about surrounding someone, all sides are protected, hidden, secured. There are no openings. In *Merriam-Webster* online dictionary, it mentions that communication is cut off from the outside. I so appreciate the idea that the enemy could not get through with his lies or perversions of the truth. The group of witnesses are those who are seeing things in heaven with the Lord right now. They are cheering for you and me. They already see the finish line and know the rewards.
- "Throw off everything that hinders"—I know that if a creature or gross object or thing startles me, I make sure to dodge or throw it off quickly. I do not want anything to injure or harm me. I need to do the same thing regarding the enemy's temptations or distractions. He loves to cause detours or hindrances from the joy that is set before me. Renewing my mind in order to focus on the things that are pure, peaceable, and full of joy is a daily process. Rather than become caught up in the temporary things

of this earth, I need to focus on the important things of life.

- "That so easily entangles"—One small incident so easily becomes a major entanglement. I trip over things that I allowed to stay in my path when I do not renew my mind continuously and focus on the things above. As He is, so am I. I need to use His truth as a machete to cut through the life-choking lies and distractions in my life. What trips me up are the things that really do not matter in the scheme of life. I need to use the light the Father promises to shine. His word is a lamp unto my feet and a light unto my path.

- "And let us run with perseverance the race marked out for us." What a mouthful! To run is to flee or escape
  - "To put off your old self, which is being corrupted by its deceitful desires; to be made new in the attitude of your minds; and to put on the new self, created to be like God in true righteousness and holiness" (Ephesians 4:22–24).

Perseverance: continuance in a state of grace to the end—this is one of my favorite thoughts. I need to be aware of the continued state of grace.

Race: onward movement, the course of life
  - "I have fought the good fight, I have finished the race, I have kept the faith" (2 Timothy 4:7).

The Lord's plans for me are different from His plans for you. You need to find out what He has marked for you. Both of us need to pursue the course of life He has for us and not detour from it. May we boldly come to His throne and inquire of His ways, His love, His solutions. Throw off the enemy's entanglements that he plans to use to choke out the Lord. Do not get caught up in the rat race. Pursue His race for you. Taste and see that the Lord is good. His mercies are new every morning. He loves you. He loves me.

Recalculating Again

While living in Germany, our family participated in various nature walks throughout the countryside, or volksmarches. Each of the major villages or cities mapped out a distinct trail, either six or twelve kilometers, for people of any age to walk. As you made the trek along the trail, there were certain checkpoints to get your paper stamped along and to enjoy a spot of hot tea and fresh brötchen bread. When you have completed the trail with your stamped paper, you received a trinket of some kind that best represented the village or city. At the end of our five-year tour of duty in Europe, we collected quite a few trinkets.

I reflected on those nature walks a great deal while thinking about how God has my steps ordered for my life. Sometimes I have taken detours, but He recalculated and opened doors to certain things in my life. How amazing that the Creator of the Earth has time to order my steps.

What exactly does that mean, to order my steps? In Exodus 13, when the pharaoh allowed the Israelites to go, they did not take the shortest route. Why? God did not want them to go through the Philistine country and be tempted to return to Egypt. Instead He ordered the steps of the Israelites through the desert toward the Red Sea. Why? He wanted them to recognize that He is Lord and to trust Him. How much trust did it take to walk through the Red Sea? Picture about a million men, women, children, livestock, and carts crossing through dry land with a wall of water on either side, deep enough to drown the enemy later. This response took a great deal of trust in order to walk out of a place with access to the known resources into a place of the unknown and, oh yes, a dead end according to many people seeing the Red Sea. It seemed impossible.

"Trust in the Lord with all your heart, and do not lean on your own understanding. In all your ways acknowledge him, and he will make straight your paths" (Proverbs 3:5–6).

"But those who hope in the LORD will renew their strength. They will soar on wings like eagles; they will run and not grow weary, they will walk and not be faint" (Isaiah 40:31).

"The steps of a man are established by the Lord, when he delights in his way" (Psalm 37:23).

"Here is what I am commanding you to do. Be strong and brave. Do not be terrified. Do not lose hope. I am the Lord your God. I will be with you everywhere you go" (Joshua 1:9).

What is your Red Sea right now? What seems impossible? He has ordered your steps, maybe not the easy or shortest way, but He has ordered your steps. He has your Promised Land prepared. He wants to know that you trust Him with the big and small decisions. He gave manna each day to the Israelites as they wandered in the desert; think about it, it's just the right quantity at just the right time. If they tried to save it for later, it became wormy and rotten. He provided for them daily as they completed their ordered steps.

He cares for you today and tomorrow. He knows what is happening to you right now. He knows the desires of your heart.

"Regerts"

It hurts to let go, but sometimes it hurts more to hold on. Random thoughts connecting to this anonymous quote:

- Controlled water release during the aftermath of Hurricane Harvey
- Release of a wounded or wild animal that recovered slowly and captured your heart
- Release of bitter feelings after a break up in a relationship
- Clearing out a closet of old clothes from another time period and sizes
- A group of so-called friends that were not true friends in time of crisis
- Feeling guilty after making a mistake that cost extensive time, money, or emotions
- Thoughts of a friend or colleague's betrayal
- Personal thoughts and emotions after a tragedy

According to an online source, Bible Reasons.com, about letting go, the author states, "What God has in store for you is never in the past." Regrets lead nowhere, only to condemnation or sadness. We know who the author of condemnation is as well as thief who comes to steal, kill, and destroy.

I am sure you have seen the Milky Way commercial with the large construction guy getting a tattoo, "No regrets." Due to the distraction of the delicious chocolate candy, the tattoo artist prints "No regerts" on his arm. Regret, according to the online dictionary means "a feeling of sadness, repentance, or disappointment over something that has happened or been done."

Dwelling on the past causes a paralysis. You spend your energy, time, and thoughts on what else could have happened if only. If you continue to look back, like Lot's wife, you cannot move forward to better or new places the Lord has for you in the big scheme of life. Why relive every moment or day of the event which consumes your joy, your hope, or replaces your dependence on a loving Father who cares about you?

Remember what the word directs you to do:

"Let your eyes look straight ahead; fix your gaze directly *before* you" (Proverbs 4:25–27).

"Brothers and sisters, I do not consider myself yet to have taken hold of it. But one thing I do: Forgetting what is behind and straining toward what is ahead, I press on toward the goal to win the prize for which God has called me heavenward in Christ Jesus" (Philippians 3:13–14).

"Forget the former things; do not dwell on the past. See, I am doing a new thing! Now it springs up; do you not perceive it? I am making a way in the wilderness and streams in the wasteland" (Isaiah 43:18–19).

It is a new day! Old things have passed away. Behold all things are new. You cannot erase the pain from the past or *unlive* something that is so real. However, the Lord is merciful to let you take the event and make you stronger in spite of it. He gives you the grace and mercy to move forward one step at a time. What the enemy meant for evil can be turned into good.

Rehearse the Goodness of God

Whenever I was growing up, there was an advertisement for a hair gel, Brylcreem, that men used. The slogan for the hair product was "A little dab will do ya." Fast forward to 2017, and there is a hip-hop dance move, dab. The move appears as if someone is sneezing and uses his/her arm to come across the face while pointing upward. Which seems more about your age, the Brylcreem or the dance move?

When you share about the *goodness of God* with someone, different views may include a promotion, passing of a test, a parking spot near the entrance of HEB, not being called on in class when you have not read the assignment, or possibly that you are released from jury duty before showing up. Bob and I have experienced a few *stories* of the goodness of God. Bear with me as I go down memory lane for a few of those special times, as we have helped different groups of people through the Isaiah 58 Ministries, our home church.

- While feeding a large group of people, food containers of spaghetti were mysteriously multiplied. We prepared around 80 or so plates and ended up feeding over 120 people. We knew exactly how many plates we prepared, yet 120 people went through the food line.
- While feeding a group of homeless people in a camp, a new person in the group requested black jeans and top for a job interview at Burger King the next morning. Bob and I had just picked up bags of clothes that someone left on the porch without any knowledge of its contents. We only knew it was the typical leftovers from yard sales. I took the young woman to our Suburban, opened the first bag of clothes. There, on top of all the clothes, a pair of black

jeans and top just her size, clean and in good condition, appeared. The two of us were amazed.

- Within three days of making the decision to help the tornado victims in Joplin, Missouri, the ministry received enough funds, materials, food, clothes, dog food, etc., to fill up a U-Haul trailer. Bob and a team of people traveled with the Holy Smoke 17-foot grill to cook for over one thousand people in need.

There are numerous other testimonies of the goodness of God in our twenty-one years of service to others together. I love to rehearse those things rather than the lies of the enemy. I need to remember the enemy wants only to steal, kill, and destroy me. He begins in my mind and then it travels through my mouth in words. Speak life. Speak the promises of God. His word is our textbook to know and understand.

Be good to your servant, God;
be as good as your Word.
Train me in good common sense;
I'm thoroughly committed to living your way.
Before I learned to answer you, I wandered all
    over the place,
but now I'm in step with your Word.
You are good, and the source of good;
train me in your goodness.
The godless spread lies about me,
but I focus my attention on what you are saying;
They're bland as a bucket of lard,
while I dance to the tune of your revelation.
My troubles turned out all for the best—
they forced me to learn from your textbook.
Truth from your mouth means more to me
than striking it rich in a gold mine. (Psalm 119:65–
    72 The Message)

He is good and is the source of good. Let Him direct your paths. Lean unto His understanding, not your own. Let Him show His goodness to you. He loves to bless His children.

Reservoir of Hope

Hope.

- I hope my grandchildren grow in the grace of Jesus Christ and know Him intimately.
- I hope each of my children walk out the destinies that God has ordained.
- I hope Christmas break is full of rest, relaxation, favor, and thankfulness with family and friends.
- I hope the two agencies award the total grant proposals for the two summer camps.

These are just of few of the many things on my list for the future. I reflect about the semester at hand and pray for the future for my family, my students, my university family, my profession, my nation, and my world. What are the things you hope that happens?

Hope means "a confident expectation and desire for something good in the future." Synonyms for the word hope are aspiration, desire, wish, expectation, ambition, aim, goal, plan, and design.

I think of hope as a treasure, something I desire to give to others who are hopeless. What are the reasons for feeling hopeless? There are probably many reasons, but I think about people who allow the whispers of the enemy to drown out the voice of the Lord and His plans for the future. On the other hand, some people feel a sense of punishment from past mistakes and think of not deserving anything better. Another view that I hear from people include, "I am not smart enough, rich enough, or lucky enough"—all about the person. I base my hope on the righteousness of Christ; He is the cornerstone, the Lord of all. It is through surrendering my plans to the Lord that my hope becomes a realization of something good in the future. The fulfillment of the hope is not within me; it is the finished work of the cross, the great exchange. There is something good in the future. The Lord promises to turn what is meant for evil into good. His mercies are new each morning. He gives grace to each of us. There is nothing too big or too small that He cannot handle. If He knows the number of hairs on my head, then He surely knows how to take care of the future.

"For I know the thoughts that I think toward you, says the LORD, thoughts of peace and not of evil, to give you a future and a hope" (Jeremiah 29:11).

"But those who hope in the Lord will renew their strength. They will soar on wings like eagles; they will run and not grow weary, they will walk and not be faint" (Isaiah 40:31).

"Now faith is confidence in what we hope for and assurance about what we do not see" (Hebrews 11:1).

"Eye has not seen, nor ear heard, nor have entered into the heart of man the things which God has prepared for those who love Him" (1 Corinthians 2:9).

Ruined: Cannot Unsee

The past several weeks included final projects, final exams, units of curriculum, and self-assessments. Many of you reading this encouraging e-mail have endured the spring semester classes or have graduated and are inflicting the same types of assignments on your students. I just received an e-mail from a current student in one of my classes, which read, "I am even more thankful to be 'ruined.'" If you have not heard me refer to being ruined, let me explain. After you understood the importance of student-centered instruction, incorporating hands-on learning, and respectful assignments, returning to traditional transmission teaching is unlikely. *Ruined* fits the description of what happened, you cannot unsee something.

This reminded me of a Georgia businessman, David Van Cronkhite. He and his wife attended a church service in Atlanta one Sunday and heard the pastor preaching about giving a cup of cold water to the least of these. Remember the verse, Matthew 25:45, "He will reply, 'Truly I tell you, whatever you did not do for one of the least of these, you did not do for me.'" David visited with the pastor after the service and asked, "Where do I find these people that you are talking about?"

The pastor invited David and Janice to lunch. They drove through Spaghetti Junction, a tangled section of interstate highways near the state capitol building. Under the bridges, huddled in various positions were the "least of these." David then stated, "I have been ruined because I can no longer unsee these people." He had never taken the time to notice life under the highways and bridges. He was busy with his appointments, real estate contracts, and growing his company. He later laid his briefcase down and raised his Bible as the most important possession while he craftily purchased an old tobacco warehouse to begin a ministry called Blood and Fire. The name of the ministry is from the Bible verses, Acts 2:18–19: "Even on My servants, both men and women, I will pour out My Spirit in those days, and they will prophesy. I will show wonders in the heavens above and signs on the earth below, blood and fire and clouds of smoke."

In what ways are you ruined for the Lord? What things can you not unsee?

- **His goodness**—Psalm 23:6: "Surely goodness and mercy shall follow me all the days of my life, and I shall dwell in the house of the Lord forever."
- **His unconditional love**—Ephesians 3:17–19: "And I pray that you, being rooted and established in love, may have power, together with all the Lord's holy people, to grasp how wide and long and high and deep is the love of Christ, and to know this love that surpasses knowledge that you may be filled to the measure of all the fullness of God."
- **His forgiveness**—Psalm 51:7, 9: "Purge me with hyssop, and I shall be clean; wash me, and I shall be whiter than snow. Hide your face from my sins, and blot out all my iniquities. Create in me a clean heart, O God, and renew a right spirit within me."
- **His peace**—John 14:27: "Peace I leave with you, My peace I give to you; not as the world gives do I give to you. Let not your heart be troubled, neither let it be afraid."
- **His hope**—Isaiah 40:31: "But those who hope in the Lord will renew their strength. They will soar on wings like eagles; they will run and not grow weary, they will walk and not be faint."
- **His righteousness**—Galatians 3:11: "Now that no one is justified by the Law before God is evident; for, the *righteous man* shall live by *faith*."

Just as David and Janice, many of the students in my classes, family members, and close friends have done, we have tasted and seen that the Lord is good (1 Peter 2:3).

See it, believe it, live it, and share it!

Star Trek: Live Long and Prosper

Space: the final frontier. These are the voyages of the
starship *Enterprise*. Its five-year mission: to explore strange
new worlds, to seek out new life and new civilizations,
to boldly go where no man has gone before.
—William Shatner

As I was meditating this week, one of the images seen in many Christmas Hallmark movies, nativity Christmas scenes on lawns, or Christmas greeting cards is the brilliant star above the stable where the infant Jesus lay wrapped in swaddling clothes. I began to read the account of the birth of Jesus. It is interesting to me how the shepherds arrived on the day of the birth (Luke 2:11) while the wise men brought gifts later to the family (Matthew 2:11).

By the time the wise men arrived, Mary; Joseph; and the toddler Jesus, around two years of age were living in a house. I thought it strange that even with the description of being wise, it took them about two years to travel the distance from the Far East to find the Messiah, and even had to ask Herod for directions. They continued to follow their GPS (glowing, pronounced star) until they found the dwelling of this special young child. The wise men unpacked the treasure sacks to bless the family with three gifts: gold (precious metal), frankincense (a perfume), and myrrh (an oil). Joseph, a carpenter, and Mary, a stay-at-home mom, probably needed the gold immediately to pay for the long journey, deposits, and relocation due to the slanderous rumors following the young couple.

What was the significance of these unique and special gifts given to the Messiah's family? Gold represents the royalty or kingship of Jesus while frankincense, an expensive resin, relates to the priestly role of Jesus connecting to healings and power of prayer. The myrrh, a sad yet prophetic gift, reflected the oil needed during death and burial ceremonies. I am sure Mary smiled with tears in her eyes as she and Joseph accepted the precious gifts.

"Now after Jesus was born in Bethlehem of Judea in the days of Herod the king, behold, magi from the east arrived in Jerusalem, saying, 'Where is He who has been born King of the Jews? For we saw His star in the east, and have come to worship Him'" (Matthew 2:1–2).

The significance of the star is amazing. Just to think it rose in the opposite sky—west—as well as moving south and led the magi to the Messiah's house. They knelt down and worshipped Him. After giving the gifts, they returned home on another route to avoid reporting to Herod.

After you encounter the Messiah, you never return home the same way. You realize the enemy is seeking whom he may devour, planning to steal, kill, and destroy, as well as blinding you with doubt, fear, and lies about who you are. Look up. Follow the Bethlehem star to the Messiah's dwelling now, which is in you. You are the temple now. Remember the gifts given to the toddler—royalty, priesthood, and salvation. You possess all that He is. Share the too good to be true news with others. Share life rather than condemnation, judgment, and death.

"But you are a chosen people, a royal priesthood, a holy nation, God's special possession, that you may declare the praises of him who called you out of darkness into his wonderful light" (1 Peter 2:9).

"Your hearts and minds must be made completely new, and you must put on the new self, which is created in God's likeness and reveals itself in the true life that is upright and holy" (Ephesians 4:23–24).

Remember the final words of Spock, a traditional Jewish blessing: "Live long and prosper." Peace be upon you.

The Current of Love

Whenever my dad passed away in 1987, I was pleasantly shocked after the memorial service. Numerous people who had worked with my dad shared various stories about how my dad had helped them through various types of traumatic events. I felt as if I was going on a character scavenger hunt through the last ten years of my dad's life. I heard more about how he ministered the love of Christ through his day-to-day encounters with people at work. After his twenty-six years in the military, he worked as a transportation director for fourteen years with the Owens-Illinois Paper Mill in South Georgia. One situation involved a coworker who did not have medical insurance for his kids and needed financial assistance for his son's surgery. As that man explained to me about my dad's gift of making the surgery possible, I remembered the many times that Dad loved to stay late and arrive early at work to meet up with people. He never spoke about the reasons. He just loved to be with people. This one story about helping with a boy's surgery was one of many stories shared to me about how my dad assisted or connected people to the best resources to make things happen. He always loved to give even when he had no money to give. Many times he acquired free turkeys, hams, boxes of fruit, or gift certificates from transportation companies desiring to get him or O and I as a constant customer. He was the king of regifting, especially during the holiday seasons. He literally was a river, he received these gifts and then transported them to those in need. He rarely kept anything for himself. The current of love flowed quietly and quickly.

Wilferd A. Peterson wrote in *The Art of Living* ([New York: Simon & Schuster, 1961], 44–45), "The art of Thanksgiving is *Thanksliving*. It is gratitude in action. It is applying Albert Schweitzer's philosophy:

'in gratitude for your own good fortune you must render in return some sacrifice of your life for the other life.'"

During the Thanksgiving season, we have an intentional day dedicated to remembering the many blessings in life. What does all your lists consist of? I encourage you to go down memory lane right now and see all that the Lord has done for you in order to bring you to today. Then as you remember what you have been given, think about all that you have given to others. You have made someone's day, year, or life. If you have listened, hugged, encouraged, or provided something for someone, you have made a difference in someone's life. It does not matter how big or small the gift of friendship or love shown; it matters. Don't miss out on honoring someone through your life.

"In everything, I showed you that by this kind of hard work we must help the weak, remembering the words of the Lord Jesus Himself: 'It is more blessed to give than to receive'" (Acts 20:35).

"You will be enriched in every way so that you can be generous on every occasion, and through us your generosity will result in thanksgiving to God" (2 Corinthians 9:11).

"Let them give thanks to the LORD for his unfailing love and his wonderful deeds for mankind, for he satisfies the thirsty and fills the hungry with good things" (Psalm 107:8–9).

Thanksgiving does not need to occur only in November. It is a lifestyle with Christ. Be thankful. Let the praise proceed from your lips. Each day is an opportunity for you. Extend a hand rather than desire a handout. Offer a shoulder rather than possess a chip on the shoulder. Provide a listening ear rather than give an earful. Let love and respect flow from your life rather than demanding to be loved and respected. Practice Thanksliving each day.

The Guardian

I lift up my eyes toward the mountains—
from where will my help come?
My help is from the Lord,
maker of heaven and earth.
He will never let your foot slip,
Nor will your guardian become drowsy.
Look! The one who is guarding Israel
never sleeps and does not take naps.
The Lord is your guardian;
the Lord is your shade at your right side.
The sun will not ravage you by day,
nor the moon by night.
The Lord will guard you from all evil,
Preserving your life.
The Lord will guard your goings and comings,
from this time on and forever.

—Psalm 121

This week's e-mail is brief. I just want to encourage you. My heart is overwhelmed with hope and excitement in what Jesus is doing in your life as well as mine. Do you realize that He cares about what you are dealing with right now? Do you understand that the creator of the universe, the one who created you in His image wants to abide in you and you in Him? Do you know that He already has your steps prepared for tomorrow and the day after that, next week, next year, and the next decade? He has plans to prosper you, to give you hope and a future. Jesus loves *you*! Do not grow weary in doing good. We go through challenges in all areas of our lives, at work, in school, with friends, and even with family. Nothing is permanent.

Do not be discouraged. Stop babbling and listen to Him. I heard a friend say one time, "The Lord cannot kiss a babbling bride." He wants to comfort you right now. You are not alone. He has not brought you this far to leave you. He can work together for good what was meant for evil. He is your advocate. He is your defender. He is a strong tower. He is your shield. As Graham Cooke says, "Ask the Lord who He wants to be for you now, that He wasn't yesterday (or whatever time frame you want to use)."

The Parade of God's Goodness

This week, I had the pleasure of listening to a few people discuss the many events our Hardin-Simmons University Six white horses participated during a fall semester. We were talking about the horses' spirits and personalities during all of the events. We were imagining what the world must look like through the eyes of each of the horses with everyone coming closer to pose for photos, to pet the muzzle or forehead, or just to cheer as the horses passed by. A good friend and colleague immediately responded, "Every day is a parade."

I began the process of connecting that statement to a Christian's life. I thought about being intentional in finding the best places to view God's handiwork in my life, to find the unique blessings in my life, to celebrate the small yet powerful miracles each day, as well as to be ready to move as the spirit leads. The parade of God's goodness.

"Surely goodness and mercy shall follow me all the days of my life, and I shall dwell in the house of the Lord forever" (Psalm 23:6).

"Every good gift and every perfect gift is from above, coming down from the Father of lights with whom there is no variation or shadow due to change" (James 1:17).

"He who dwells in the shelter of the Most High will abide in the shadow of the Almighty. I will say to the Lord, "My refuge and my fortress, my God, in whom I trust." For he will deliver you from the snare of the fowler and from the deadly pestilence. He will cover you with his pinions, and under his wings you will find refuge; his faithfulness is a shield and buckler. You will not fear the terror of the night, nor the arrow that flies by day" (Psalm 91:1–16).

In my 21,900-day parade, I have numerous testimonies of God's goodness. As my mother said in our last phone conversation, "The Lord has been good to me." For me, the parade of goodness included His gift of salvation; His unconditional love; His promises of refuge and protection; and His demonstrations of love in family, friends, colleagues, students, even strangers or angels, as well as His vow of staying with me no matter what. Other floats contained the tough times that I knew God was there, providing peace in the storm, strength to endure, and joy rather than mourning. His invisible hugs enveloped me; His Spirit guided me and even lifted me out of the pits of depression. What a parade!

How does your parade look? Is it a parade? On the other hand, do you view your life right now as a circular horse ride at the fair? It is time to celebrate God's goodness. Break away.

The Veranda of Love

In 1990, I wrote a story entitled "Spots on the Porch," about my life growing up as a child, teenager, and young adult. I was reminded of that special place today while teaching in one of my classes. I won't bore you with the entire literary work, but I want to share a few things about this sentimental place. It was not so much the actual location, as it was when the people in my life were together on the porch, I felt safe and loved. The medium-sized porch was large enough to have about five or six white rocking chairs, a few potted plants, and lots of space to move around into different groupings to visit; to be on the lookout for guests; or to just simply rest and stare at the beautiful landscape, the sky, or even the rain as it pelted through the pine trees and azalea shrubs. My dad loved our front porch. He enjoyed rocking and drinking sweet tea while resting from all of the yardwork. The many times that I helped him with mowing, raking, or edging, we always ended up collapsing on the porch before entering the house. It was a special place to hear stories of him growing up, or he would retell something that we did as a family while traveling around because of the military. After getting married and having a family, the front porch was a cemented playground for the grandchildren to play chase, to climb between the shrubs and the porch, or to rock in the chair to the very edge of the porch, daring gravity to plunge them into the yard. Later, when we moved away to Mississippi and Germany, the porch was the first and last places my parents would stand while greeting us or sending us on our way home. The porch was a gathering place for short spurts of love, acceptance, laughter, and even tears. My last memory of that special porch involved the many relatives and close friends who attended my dad's funeral in 1987. We ended up sitting outside, telling stories about him. To me, that was the memorial service for my dad rather than the formal one at the funeral home. The spots on the porch meant a great deal to me then and even now.

According to the Merriam Webster Online Dictionary, a porch is a sheltered area at the entrance to a building. I always had a sense of protection under that special porch, or maybe it was because my dad was there with me. I began to meditate about the sheltered area. I found a few verses that touched my heart about safety, shelter, and strength during times of stress, fear, anxiety, or sadness.

"Those who go to God Most High for safety will be protected by the Almighty. I will say to the Lord, "You are my place of safety and protection. You are my God and I trust you." God will save you from hidden traps and from deadly diseases. He will cover you with his feathers, and under his wings you can hide. His truth will be your shield and protection" (Psalm 91:1–4).

"For thou hast been a strength to the poor, a strength to the needy in his distress, a refuge from the storm, a shadow from the heat, when the blast of the terrible ones is as a storm against the wall" (Isaiah 25:4).

"There will be a shelter to give shade from the heat by day, and refuge and protection from the storm and the rain" (Isaiah 4:6).

If you needed a place to retreat and tune out the sounds of the world in order to focus on the voice of the Lord, where would you go? Some of our students may find solace in the university library, others may go recline in a hammock by the university pond, a few of you may sit in your favorite place to view the Lord's creation—the mountains, the beach, a field of cows grazing, or possibly just go fishing. Find that place to be sheltered or protected by the rush around you. We all need to be reminded of who is taking care of us. He holds the world together by the power of His words. He loves you and cares about everything you are experiencing right now. He sees His plans for you, those plans are to build a hope and a future. He has not forgotten you. He wants you to come rock on the front porch of your life with Him.

Tides of Mercy

The last time my husband Bob and I visited Biloxi, Mississippi, we rode along the beach on Highway 90. Most of the time, the tide was out. It exposed a great deal of the ocean floor of the Gulf of Mexico. We recalled the stories of life after Hurricane Katrina, when there were 18-wheelers, cars, washing machines, various parts of casinos and housing exposed along the shore with waves of debris hitting from all sides. Along the Gulf Coast remnants of the past dotted the shoreline with the hustle and bustle of recovery teams assisting those in need.

Immediately, communities came together to assess the damage and make decisions of the most urgent needs to the less urgent. People worked together in times of distress. They assisted with whatever they had—water bottles, generators, tools to remove obstacles, or even just hugs as people saw their lives floating away. The recovery teams came from all parts of the world to offer physical labor, comfort, food, shelter, or whatever they could do. In times of disaster or pain, people become more like family.

Fast forward to 2018. Hurricane—(you name it). Different people in those areas in school, work, church, or home are in need of recovery teams. The winds and waves have destroyed bank accounts, marriages, families, jobs, friendships, family relations, and even physical bodies. According to the online *Merriam-Webster* dictionary, *debris* means the remains of something broken down or destroyed. People have visible evidence of things broken down or destroyed in their lives.

Tides of mercy are needed. Everyone is searching for some type of recovery team—someone who understands, listens and doesn't judge from the exposed debris left behind after the storms of bad decisions, immaturity, peer pressures, or just ignorance. We all need people to listen, to love, and to be the hands and feet of Jesus. We do not need appraisers to come along and tell us the value of the debris and where we went wrong in the storm. We need those people who share the good news about the one who replaces, restores, completes, heals, and vindicates all of those who call upon the name of Jesus. We need people in our lives to proclaim the hope, a positive, confident expectation of good. Who is the source of that hope? You know.

"Let us then approach God's throne of grace with confidence, so that we may receive mercy and find grace to help us in our time of need" (Hebrews 4:16).

"Praise be to the God and Father of our Lord Jesus Christ! In his great mercy he has given us new birth into a living hope through the resurrection of Jesus Christ from the dead" (1 Peter 1:3).

Tides of mercy—great visual. I see the washing away of so much right now and never more to be seen as the word of God refers to sin as far as the east is from the west. We all need the high tide of mercy in our lives and to pay it forward. Clean up our perspectives, do not focus on what the storm actually did. View the restoration process and finished work at the cross. The Lord does not see the debris any longer. His blood covers it all. It is written!

Timing

Picture this—yes, I might sound a bit like Dorothy's mom, Sophia, in *The Golden Girls*. My husband, Bob, is traveling alone on Thanksgiving night from Abilene, Texas, to central Georgia to attend his uncle's funeral. Our family's schedules prevent all of us from going with Bob. East of Shreveport, Los Angeles, the good old Oldsmobile breaks down on the side of the highway. Bob lifts the hood, trying to be Mr. Goodwrench, and soon discovers a destroyed and detached hose from some important parts in the engine (I am writing this without Bob's help as you can see). Bob is stuck in the middle of nowhere late at night or early in the morning. At that time, we did not possess any cell phones. He sits in the car and just prays for help. All of a sudden, an elderly man drives up and stops in front of the Oldsmobile. He offers Bob assistance. He is a mechanic, or should I say, MacGyver (for those of you who do not remember this weekly TV show, look it up on YouTube). He has a few materials in his car that he immediately constructs an unusual solution to get Bob on the road again. He refuses any pay. The man came out of nowhere and then suddenly disappears.

"Trust in the LORD with all your heart, and lean not on your own understanding; in all your ways acknowledge Him, and He shall direct your paths" (Proverbs 3:5–6).

Another picture: Bob and I visit homeless camps on Friday and Saturday nights several years ago. One particular Friday afternoon, as Bob prepares the Cajun chicken entrée in his Cajun cookers, a friend calls to let us know about leftover clothes from a previous yard sale. She asks us if we could offer the clothes to people in need. We say,

"Absolutely." She delivers about six or seven huge black trash bags of clothes. We place all of the bags in the back of our Suburban to be delivered the next day. We look at the clock and realize that we need to be on our way to Cherokee's camp; we know there might be around twenty people waiting on dinner. We quickly inventoried all of our supplies—water bottles, desserts, etc. We arrive and begin to unload all of the dinner. It is almost like a Walton's Mountain dinner scene; everyone quickly dipping the servings, finding their favorite places around the campfire, and saying grace. Indian John throws his hat down on the ground and falls to his knees. He screams out the prayer. I know the Lord is smiling or maybe even laughing at this point. As everyone is eating the spicy chicken rice dish, a new young female arrives to eat. Everyone knows her except Bob and me. She sits down across from me and begins to tell everyone that she has a job interview at Burger King the next morning. However, she states, "I can't go because I do not own a pair of black jeans." Those six or seven black trash bags of clothes come to my mind. I suddenly say, "I am not sure what we have in the back of our Suburban, but you are welcome to look through the clothes that were given to us this afternoon." She and I walk to the Suburban and open the first bag. What do we discover? A pair of black jeans (in good condition) that were just her size. The two of us hug one another with thankful hearts.

"Ask, and it will be given to you; seek, and you will find; knock, and it will be opened to you." (Matthew 7:7)

I have many other pictures of God's goodness, but I end with this particular one. Bob and I marry in my sophomore year and he was in his junior year of undergraduate school at Valdosta State College (now it is a university). If you want a good chuckle, ask me about how we met and developed our relationship through phone calls for the first month or so. Anyway, Bob enters the military, making about $100 a week before taxes after our wedding, and I bring home whatever minimum wage is for a student-worker in the Dewar School of Education. We did not have a phone, a television, a record player, or a radio. We balance our checkbook and discover that we have $1.87 as our balance. Right beside the checkbook is a bill that we need to pay by the end of the week. We rule out the options of asking our parents, who live in the same town, selling my accordion, or selling plasma. We pray for wisdom and favor. Two days later, Bob checks our mail. He tells me that a long-time friend of his parents' military years sent us something. He pulls the card out of the envelope, and a check falls into his lap. He picks up the check while he reads the card aloud to me, "Butch, I'm sorry that we did not attend your wedding two years ago, but I felt like sending you a little something to wish you the very best." Yes, you know what he sent us, the exact amount of what our bill was.

"God is our refuge and strength, a very present help in trouble" (Psalm 46:1).

Notice the previous scripture states "present" help. He is with us each step of the way. He does not love us conditionally. He is present with you and me right now. He knows exactly the plan He has for us, to give a hope and future. It is about His timing and ways of helping us. "He uses the foolish things to confound the wise" (1 Corinthians 1:27). He uses His word, circumstances, and people to assist us. His angels are all around us.

Tokens of His Mercy

In our early years of the marriage, Bob's job in the USAF required him to be gone on temporary duty (TDY) a good bit. During one of the lengthier periods of his absence, I felt like everything was crashing down around me. Some of the hats I wore included a full-time teacher, mother, church pianist, member of three school parent-teacher organizations, and graduate student working on my master's in education degree. One particular week, our next-door neighbor, who I had never met before, came over to complain that our watchdog was barking too much. I felt a combination of joy and frustration, happy that our dog was alert to sounds/smells around our backyard and upset that our neighbor chose that night to introduce herself to me about our dog. As the week progressed, one of our three kids had a sudden stomach bug attack, which we all shared the next day. The week continued with little opportunity for sleep. Later that week, all three kids were playing and irritating each other while continuing to call me into the room to settle debates over the issues at hand. I felt overwhelmed at that point and yelled, "I do not speak!" while pointing to all three of them. What I had intended to say was "I am not going to say this again." As quickly as the words escaped my lips, laughter erupted. Everything calmed down. All three of the kids, who are adults now, have reminded me of that story numerous times, as they have children now who have driven them to sputter crazy things too.

As the semester has developed into our fourth week, I have thought about how easily I have allowed things to overwhelm me just like that four-year period when Bob was gone. I have allowed these things—people, deadlines, reports, schedules, or the outside things to invade and take up space in my mind and heart. These things have tried to rob me of the things that I know are pure, peaceable, and full of truth. I have posted Bible verses in various places to remind me of His ways, His thoughts about me, His plans to prosper me and to give me hope and a future. All I need to do is listen and obey.

"God means what he says. What he says goes. His powerful Word is sharp as a surgeon's scalpel, cutting through everything, whether doubt or defense, laying us open to listen and obey. Nothing and no one is impervious to God's Word. We can't get away from it—no matter what" (Hebrews 4:12–13).

"No, in all these things we are more than conquerors through Him who loved us. For I am convinced that neither death nor life, neither angels nor principalities, neither the present nor the future, nor any powers, neither height nor depth, nor anything else in all creation, will be able to separate us from the love of God that is in Christ Jesus our Lord" (Romans 8: 37–39).

"'No weapon that is formed against you will prosper; and every tongue that accuses you in judgment you will condemn. This is the heritage of the servants of the LORD, and their vindication is from Me,' declares the LORD" (Isaiah 54:17).

> They who dwell in the ends of the earth stand in
>   awe of Your signs;
> You make the dawn and the sunset shout for joy.
> You visit the earth and cause it to overflow;
> You greatly enrich it;
> The stream of God is full of water;
> You prepare their grain, for thus You prepare the
>   earth.
>
> You water its furrows abundantly,
> You settle its ridges,
> You soften it with showers,
> You bless its growth.

You have crowned the year with Your bounty,
And Your paths drip with fatness. (Psalm 65:8–11)

I desire for my life to be crowned with His bounty and my paths to drip with fatness. I looked up *fatness*, to ensure that I did desire this. I found the following commentary (Bible Hub website): "*Fatness*—Wherever God goes, speaking after the manner of men, or works, He leaves the tokens of His mercy behind Him; He dispenses rich and salutary blessings, and thus makes His paths to shine after Him."

He leaves the tokens of His mercy behind Him!

Toxic Waste: A Blast
from the Past

We lived in Wiesbaden, Germany, from 1985 to 1989. Many of you probably did not hear about the Chernobyl Disaster on April 26, 1986, at the Chernobyl Nuclear Power Plant near Pripyat, in what was then part of the Ukrainian Soviet Socialist Republic of the Soviet Union (USSR). However, we have vivid memories of that catastrophe. For nine days, a "fire" produced updrafts of radioactive material equal in magnitude to products released from an explosion in the power plant into the atmosphere. The fallout extended through western USSR and Europe. The blast caused two deaths within the power plant, and later, twenty-nine firefighters and employees died in the days to months afterward from acute radiation syndrome. Other people dealt with the potential for long-term cancer. In Europe, we did not eat fresh vegetables, meat from animals grazing, or fresh fish from the lakes or rivers. The children did not play outside on the grass. Everyone stayed inside as much as possible. We examined everything and followed every instruction from the health and government officials.

Toxic (according to the online *Merriam-Webster* dictionary):

- containing or being poisonous material especially when capable of causing death or serious debilitation
- extremely harsh, malicious, or harmful

Satan is extremely harsh, malicious, and harmful either immediately or after the fact. Yet sometimes, he is the counterfeit and seems appealing, popular, and fulfilling. He enjoys stealing, killing, or destroying those who oppose him. He uses the principalities of the world to deceive or confuse people who believe in the Christ, the Son of the living God. He is nonstop, continuous in our weakest areas. Sometimes it is a direct blast, other times it is the residue left on familiar things or people. How do you prevent the damage?

"Above all else, *guard your heart*, for everything you do flows from it" (Proverbs 4:23).

Recently, I have thought a great deal about guarding your heart because of the many outside influences that may seem innocent, popular, or rationale. The types of things that I have allowed into my temple influence my words, actions, and deeds. What preventative measures did I make to avoid a "blast from a nuclear power plant"?

"And the peace of God, which surpasses all understanding, will guard your hearts and minds through Christ Jesus…whatever is true, whatever is noble, whatever is right, whatever is pure, whatever is lovely, whatever is admirable – if anything is excellent or worthy of praise— think about these things" (Philippians 4:7–8).

"Do not allow this world to mold you in its own image. Instead, be transformed from the inside out by renewing your mind. As a result, you will be able to discern what God wills and whatever God finds good, pleasing, and complete" (Romans 12:2).

"The good man brings good things out of the good treasure of his heart, and the evil man brings evil things out of the evil treasure of his heart. For out of the overflow of the heart, the mouth speaks" (Luke 6:45).

Guard (definitions from *Merriam-Webster* online dictionary):

- to keep safe from harm or danger; protect; watch over

- to provide or equip with some safeguard or protective appliance, as to prevent loss, injury, etc.
- to position oneself so as to obstruct or impede the movement or progress of (an opponent on offense)

Synonyms:

shield, shelter, preserve, defender, protector; watchman, guardian; sentinel, patrol, defense, protection, security, safety; bulwark.

How many Bible verses just came to your mind while reading the synonyms?

"The LORD is my rock and my fortress and my deliverer, My God, my rock, in whom I take refuge; My shield and the horn of my salvation, my stronghold" (Psalm 18:2).

"You are my defender and protector; I put my hope in your promise" (Psalm 18:2).

"He will cover you with His pinions, And under His wings you may seek refuge; His faithfulness is a shield and bulwark" (Psalm 91:4).

Guard your heart. Speak life, not death. Speak words of edification, exhortation, and comfort to those around you. Cover your ears from lies, insults, fear, and doubt. Take cover from the fallout from the enemy. He is defeated. As a friend said tonight in our church group, we have read the final chapter and we have won.

You Are Invited

One of our good friends is an Italian New Yorker from Brooklyn. He and his wife have shared numerous family stories with Bob and me through our many years of friendship. One time, Pete showed us a few family photos of his family eating a holiday meal when he was a young boy. Bob and I were impressed that at least fifteen people were crowded around this small table happily eating pasta and sharing stories. Pete explained how it was normal for all the family to eat in the kitchen area in his home. His mother, Connie, was an outstanding cook, as well as all the family members contributing to the meal. Notice how many times I mentioned *family*. The thoughts of being related or kin were gathered together.

Early in Bob's military career, a supervisor hosted an office dinner party at his home. The spouses were invited to attend. Once we arrived and mingled with all the people attending the dinner, the hosts guided everyone into a huge dining area with a massive table that extended the length of the dining room. To me, the table was close to 15 feet in length. There was no way to hear all the conversations at the table, let alone to tell a story so everyone could hear. You spoke to the nearest person or stranger to you. The supervisor had wait staff passing out the plates of food, drinks, and desserts. It was more formal than intimate. There were no deep relationships. It was only surface chatter, the weather, places you lived, your jobs, etc.

For a brief period, our family of five lived in a small rental home. The floor plan of the house was not the best. The dining room near the kitchen was tiny, too small for our dining room table. It was so small, we ate on TV trays in the den for a while. One day, our baby daughter mentioned that we needed more intimate family time with a table. Bob and I both agreed but knew it would be an interesting time together in the small space. We moved our table into that tiny space close to the kitchen to enjoy the conversations, stories, and daily face-to-face encounters with each other. It was like the Walton's family (yes, I know this is an older TV show that many of you have never seen unless on *Nick at Nite*) dining in an elevator. We were related; we were a family gathered together.

Tables—a piece of furniture, a meeting place, or a place of getting together. The menus may change, but the people around the table come together to build relationships. In modern times, people sit up straight at the table using various types of chairs or benches. In the early Jewish times, it was okay to stretch out and recline at the table. The meals lasted longer, depending on the celebrations, the topics, etc. The table was the location to bring people together for a common cause, extended blessings (i.e., in relationships, physically, spiritually, etc.).

Just think about two major table times in the Bible, one in the Old Testament; Passover (the feast of unleavened bread in individual homes with the doorposts covered with blood of spotless lambs) and the other in the New Testament, the Last Supper (communion—upper room, Jesus and disciples, speaking of the blood and body of the lamb that would be slain). Both meals brought freedom and life, One required annual visits to the temple and the priest, and the other was, once and for all, based upon the lamb of God, Jesus. There is one table we have not witnessed yet, the marriage table with our groom, Jesus. We, the church, His bride have a future feast to enjoy celebrating and praising Him forever.

All the tables bring family together; we are kin. It doesn't matter what career, what age, what level of education, when you come to the table, your past is forgotten; you enter the world of grace. Taste and see that the Lord is good (Psalm 34:8).

Here are a few more verses about the table or about dining:

"When the time came, Jesus and the apostles sat down together at the table" (Luke 22:14).

"When He had reclined at the table with them, He took the bread and blessed it, and breaking it, He began giving it to them" (Luke 24:30).

"As they were reclining at the table and eating, Jesus said, "Truly I say to you that one of you will betray Me—one who is eating with Me" (Mark 14:18).

"Then it happened that as Jesus was reclining at the table in the house, behold, many tax collectors and sinners came and were dining with Jesus and His disciples" (Matthew 9:10).

"You prepare a table before me in the presence of my enemies. You anoint my head with oil; my cup overflows" (Psalm 23:5).

"Then the angel said to me, 'Write this: Blessed are those who are invited to the wedding supper of the Lamb!' And he added, 'These are the true words of God'" (Revelation 19:9).

Think about the people who ate with Jesus—the religious, the broken, the poor, the faithful, the Gentiles. He prepared the table for the world to dine. "For God did not send his Son into the world to condemn the world, but to save the world through him" (John 3:17). Think about the message shared at the table—His plans; His prediction of betrayal; His love for the people; and His command "as oft as you do this, do this in remembrance of me"; and His words, "Neither do I condemn you, go and sin no more" (John 8:11). He asked questions, spoke in parables, used inanimate objects to teach lessons, and touched people. The table was a key place to meet the world.

You are cordially invited to.　　　•

Why-Fi

You are an amazing creation. You have a purpose. You may not fully see the entire picture of how God sees you, but you are taking steps each day to encounter exactly all that you are to do.

> He who has a why to live for can bear almost any how.
> —Friedrich Nietzsche

"My frame was not hidden from you when I was made in the secret place, when I was woven together in the depths of the earth. Your eyes saw my unformed body; all the days ordained for me were written in your book before one of them came to be" (Psalm 139:15–16).

"But I have raised you up for this very purpose, that I might show you my power and that my name might be proclaimed in all the earth" (Exodus 9:16).

"Many are the plans in a person's heart, but it is the Lord's purpose that prevails" (Proverbs 19:21).

"And we know that in all things God works for the good of those who love him, who have been called according to his purpose" (Romans 8:28).

As Simon Sinek says, "Begin with the why." Understand your why. Then you have a reason to see the steps, the how and the what in your life, the process of how God plans to bring it all together. He is leading you day by day. Remember His word is a lamp on your feet and a light unto your path. He wants you to trust in Him not yourself.

He delights in you. His mercies are new every morning. He sees you through Christ's finished work at the cross. You do not have to perform for His love. He loves you. You now possess unmerited favor, His grace. He wants you to be His hands and feet. He wants you to proclaim the good news in the marketplace. Where are you now? This is the place to share His love. He wants you to focus on Him first, and then He gives you the desires of your heart (because He places those desires in your heart).

Begin with the why! You have a purpose. Listen to His voice. He is speaking. Connect to His Why-Fi! He desires to be your server.

About the Author

B. Renee Collins, Ph.D. experienced extensive travels around the globe as a daughter of a twenty-six-year US military veteran and, later, as a spouse of a twenty-one-year US military veteran. As a lifelong learner, she pursued a career of sharing hope to the hopeless through public school teaching. She completed her bachelor of science in education at Valdosta State University, Valdosta, Georgia. After a decade of traveling and teaching in places like Biloxi, Mississippi, and a Department of Defense School in Wiesbaden, Germany, she then transitioned to West Texas because of her husband's military assignment. Continuing to find out more about unlocking the hearts and minds of struggling learners, she completed a master of education reading specialist at Hardin-Simmons University in Abilene, Texas. Her doctor of philosophy in curriculum and instruction was later completed at Texas Tech University in Lubbock, Texas. The professional relationships with her HSU graduate faculty members later opened the door to teaching future teachers and university professors how to motivate and reach diverse learners with effective pedagogical practices. With twenty years in public education and almost twenty years in higher education, Dr. Collins has advanced to professor of education at Hardin-Simmons University and associate dean of the Irvin School of Education in the College of Human Sciences and Educational Studies at HSU in Abilene, Texas. She and her husband have three children and five grandchildren whom she revels in being their Nay-Nay.